Human Rights Interventions

Series Editors
Chiseche Mibenge, Stanford University, Stanford, CA, USA
Irene Hadiprayitno, Leiden University, Leiden, Zuid-Holland,
The Netherlands

The traditional human rights frame creates a paradigm by which the duty bearer's (state) and rights holder's (civil society organizations) interests collide over the limits of enjoyment and enforcement. The series departs from the paradigm by centering peripheral yet powerful actors that agitate for intervention and influence in the (re)shaping of rights discourse in the midst of grave insecurities. The series privileges a call and response between theoretical inquiry and empirical investigation as contributors critically assess human rights interventions mediated by spatial, temporal, geopolitical and other dimensions. An interdisciplinary dialogue is key as the editors encourage multiple approaches such as law and society, political economy, historiography, legal ethnography, feminist security studies, and multi-media.

Samadia Sadouni

Religious Transnationalism and Climate Change

The Role of Non-State Actors

Samadia Sadouni
Sciences Po Lyon - University
of Lyon
Lyon, France

Human Rights Interventions
ISBN 978-3-031-10609-5   ISBN 978-3-031-10610-1   (eBook)
https://doi.org/10.1007/978-3-031-10610-1

This Palgrave Macmillan imprint is published by the registered company Springer Nature Switzerland AG
The registered company address is: Gewerbestrasse 11, 6330 Cham, Switzerland

Acknowledgements

The idea for this manuscript arose when I was appointed a lecturer at Sciences Po Lyon in 2012 and more specifically when I presented the course on the sociology of international relations. This helped me to analyse the role of religion in international relations in a new research project on religious actors and climate change that I also described in a volume for my « diplôme d'habilitation à diriger des recherches (HDR) » obtained in 2020 at the University of Lyon 2. I would like to thank colleagues Gilles Pollet, Roman Loimeier and Jean-Louis Marie for their fruitful comments and discussions on this research on the international political sociology of religious actors. The project «Climate Change, Migration, Governance (Security) » that I present at Sciences Po Lyon and funded by the Région Auvergne Rhône Alpes has also allowed me an opportunity to develop this research and interview climate experts and religious actors during my field trips in South Africa and subsequently online as result of the COVID-19 pandemic restrictions.

My appreciation is also addressed to Edwin Hees for the editing of my English manuscript. I want to thank the Palgrave Macmillan team, Anca Pucsa, Abarna Antonyraj and Chitra Gopalraj, for their support in preparing the publication.

Of course, any remaining mistakes in the book are my own. This is the first step in a broader research project that I intend to pursue in political sociology.

CONTENTS

1 Introduction: Religious Actors and Climate Change   1
  Outline of the Chapters   3
  Religion and State Climate Policies   8

2 Cosmopolitanism in Globalisation and New Forms
  of Transnational Religious Mobilisation   11
  Non-State Actors and Changes in World Politics   11
  Transnational Social Field   14

3 Religions from the Field of Development to Climate
  Change   25
  *Climate and International Relations: Nexus of Climate
  Change, Environment and Development*   32

4 Religious Actions to Address Climate Change: The
  International Platform   51
  Positions Taken on the Eve of COP 21- Paris Agreement 53
  Climate Justice   57
  Prevention, Mitigation and Adaptation to Climate Change 62

5 Climate Action, Religion and Civil Society in South
  Africa   71
  *African National Congress (ANC): Dialogue of Religions
  and Public Policy*   73

SAFCEI: Cooperation, Tensions and Reconciliation Between the Environmental Faith-Based NGO Sector and the State   79

6   **Conclusion: Towards Convergence**   91

Index   95

Introduction: Religious Actors and Climate Change

2015 may be regarded as a historical year for climate negotiations and sustainable development with the adoption first of Agenda 2030 and then the Paris Agreement. It was also an important milestone for religious actors involved in the international domain of global warming, now scientifically acknowledged as anthropogenic, meaning that human influence has warmed the atmosphere, the oceans and the land,[1] which in turn has environmental, economic, social and political consequences. In this book, I will examine the nature and possible influence of religion on the international agenda on climate change by adopting a perspective derived from international political sociology,[2] which includes a socio-historical analysis. Religion is understood and analysed in its plurality of confessional expressions and as functioning in the context of interfaith dialogue

---

[1] See IPCC (Intergovernmental Panel on Climate Change), 2021: Summary for Policymakers. In: Climate Change 2021: The Physical Science Basis. Contribution of Working Group I to the Sixth Assessment Report of the Intergovernmental Panel on Climate Change [Masson-Delmotte, V., P. Zhai, A. Pirani, S.L. Connors, C. Péan, S. Berger, N. Caud, Y. Chen, L. Goldfarb, M.I. Gomis, M. Huang, K. Leitzell, E. Lonnoy, J.B.R. Matthews, T.K. Maycock, T. Waterfield, O. Yelekçi, R. Yu, and B. Zhou (eds.)] in press.

[2] D. Bigo & R.B.J. Walker, "Political Sociology and the Problem of the International", *Millennium. Journal of International Studies*, 35 (3), 2007, pp. 725–739. Guillaume Devin, *Sociologie des relations internationales*, Paris, La Découverte, 2013.

© The Author(s), under exclusive license to Springer Nature Switzerland AG 2022
S. Sadouni, *Religious Transnationalism and Climate Change,*
Human Rights Interventions,
https://doi.org/10.1007/978-3-031-10610-1_1

1

through the mobilisation of diverse religious actors. Religion—as non-state actors—cannot be separated or dissociated from the transformation of the international system towards multilateralism and vice versa.[3] As opposed to the tide of theories of secularisation[4] that view religion as strictly separated from the political field and consigned to a marginal role, religion is considered here as part of internationalisation processes that we need to contextualise in order to better understand the role of religious actors in addressing climate change. A new mode of religious transnationalism has developed strongly since the 1990s and is mostly linked to international relations shaped by intergovernmental relations. Non-state actors' transnationalism in multilateral forums such as the United Nations Framework Convention on Climate Change (UNFCCC) and in the field of international public policies can therefore represent a new trend in political globalisation from below. Global governance in the field of climate change more generally is increasingly the site where we can observe globalisation in its intricate social, religious, political and economic dimensions.

The religious actors whose mobilisation and discourse are studied in this volume belong to different faiths and denominations: Christians (Catholic, Anglican and Orthodox), Muslims (mostly Sunnis) and Buddhists. However, religious transnationalism in favour of mitigating climate change is represented by various other faiths (Hinduism, Judaism, Bahaism, African traditional religions) that all have in common the protection of the environment as part of their theological and moral values.[5] The term religious actors or transnational religious actors here covers

---

[3] About a global religious resurgence and «post-secular» international relations, see Thomas, Scott M., *The Global Transformation of Religion and the Transformation of International Relations. The Struggle for the Soul of the Twenty-First Century*, New York and Basingstoke, Palgrave Macmillan, 2005; Toft, Monica Duffy, Daniel Philpott, & Timothy Samuel Shah, *God's Century. Resurgent Religion and Global Politics*, New York and London, W. W. Norton and Company, 2011; J. Haynes, "Religion and International Relations: What Are the Issues?", *International Politics*, 41, September 2004, pp. 451–462.

[4] P. L. Berger, *The Sacred Canopy: Elements of Sociological Theory of Religion*, New York, Anchor, 1969. P.L. Berger will review his earlier work and theory of secularisation. See P. L Berger, *The Desecularization of the World. Resurgent Religion and World Politics*, Eerdmans, 1999.

[5] Ralph Tanner & Colin Mitchell, *Religion and the Environment*, New York, Palgrave, 2002.

non-state entities that have the legitimacy to interpret religion based on tradition and even charisma. As this multilateral forum of the UNFCCC and especially its Conferences of the Parties is mostly an intergovern- mental space for the global governance of climate change, the religious actors who can have an impact on climate discourse and policies in these multilateral platforms are mostly faith/church leaders.

This book is the result of research initiated in 2013 and is based on interviews conducted with religious actors in South Africa and in Europe. This was done especially during an international conference co-organised at the University of Lyon on 23–24 November 2015, which is one of the rare events in the international academic sphere held during the year 2015[6] in which several religious actors (Christian, Muslim and Buddhist) participated to convey their views on climate change as part of a future international accord, which became the Paris Agreement, before going to participate in COP 21 in Paris. An international political sociology perspective has been adopted in order to study how religious actors, as non-state actors, have played a part in promoting the cause of climate mitigation and sustainable development,[7] as they are interlinked (see Chapter 3).

OUTLINE OF THE CHAPTERS

Proactive policies to mitigate global warming are at the heart of a universal discourse on climate: this is a matter of saving the planet, not only humanity. This planetary dimension, or "Mother Earth", the expres- sion used by the United Nations itself, takes into account the tremendous changes that humanity has induced in shaping the environment. The Anthropocene is the term used to focus on the evidence that humanity has had a detrimental impact on nature,[8] but it is also linked to the devel- opment of new ethical and moral debates on our way of life at the heart

[6] This international conference led to the publication of a special issue: Philippe Martin & Samadia Sadouni (eds.), «Acteurs religieux et changements climatiques», *Histoire, monde & cultures religieuses*, 2016, n° 40 (December 2016), pp. 7–121.

[7] Although religious actors of different faiths have developed climate-oriented action for more than three decades, this has become a theme in the media only since 2018.

[8] W. Steffen, P.J. Crutzen, & J.R. McNeill., "The Anthropocene: Are Humans Now Overwhelming the Great Forces of Nature?", *Ambio*, 36, 2007, pp. 614–621. For researchers and activists, "widespread and rapid changes in the atmosphere, ocean, cryosphere and biosphere have occurred. The scale of recent changes across the climate

of definitions of being and belonging. What does it mean to be human in the Anthropocene? What does it mean to belong to planet Earth, "our Mother", today and tomorrow? These questions and debates are also addressed by religious actors on the basis of their traditions informed by science and their commitment to human rights and social justice.[9] A moral commitment to respect for humanity and the planet is the channel for changing one's attitude to the outside world, leading to collective action for change.[10]

Since a constructive relationship with the Other is indispensable for efficient climate action, religious actors in the case at hand cannot formulate a discourse on the international scene in a vacuum, targeting only their respective congregations. As a matter of fact, climate is an issue that today does not only concern us all, but crucially future generations as well. Religion in this specific context thus becomes a cosmopolitan force[11] that, in the case of global climate action, encourages interfaith mobilisation, which in turn contributes to strengthening the power of religions on the international scene (see Chapter 2).

Climate change also and above all refers to the issue of sustainable development, a feature often mentioned in the Paris Agreement. How can a new sustainable political and economic organisation be implemented that is based on a new relationship between humankind and the environment? The implementation of the Paris Agreement, which is a legally binding international treaty on climate change, is based on economic and social transformation[12]: a new way of living on Planet Earth. The religious actors with whom I was able to engage consider that it is above

system as a whole and the present state of many aspects of the climate system are unprecedented over many centuries to many thousands of years". Quoted from the document entitled "Why Nature ? Why Now ? How nature is key to achieving a 1.5 °C world". The Food and Land Use Coalition, October 2021. https://www.foodandlandusecoalition. org/why-nature/.

[9] Larry L. Rasmussen, "From Social Justice to Creation Justice in the Anthropocene", in John Hart (ed.), *The Wiley Blackwell Companion to Religion and Ecology*, Hoboken, NJ, John Wiley & Sons, 2017, pp. 239–255.

[10] Margaret Ledwith, *Community Development. A Critical Approach*, chapter 5 "Collective Action for Change", Bristol, Policy Press, 2011.

[11] Ulrich Beck, "The Cosmopolitan Society and Its Enemies", *Theory, Culture and Society*, 19 (1–2), 2002, pp. 17-44; U. Beck, "The Cosmopolitan Perspective: Sociology of the Second Age of Modernity", *British Journal of Sociology*, 51(1), 2008, pp. 79–105.

[12] https://unfccc.int/process-and-meetings/the-paris-agreement/the-paris-agreement.

all a religious and moral obligation "to repent" of human activities that continue to jeopardise the planet in the present and for future generations. I will come back to this last point in the following chapters and especially in Chapter 3, which will deal more specifically with the matter of development.

Meanwhile, it is important to emphasise that climate and development have been intrinsically linked and finally internationally institutionalised since the adoption of the UN Sustainable Development Goals (SDGs) and the Paris Agreement in the same year, 2015. However, when it comes to the topic of development, the analysis becomes more complex, since the idea of development is a construct that produces its theories by borrowing from other social fields such as academia, politics, culture, religion and business.[13] It can therefore be concluded that development simultaneously produces a world as well as knowledge about that world. The knowledge on constructing the sustainable world of today is also analysed here as being formed through a set of interactions in the *transnational climate field*[14] (Chapter 2) that needs to be examined by studying the discourses and modes of cooperation between development actors from various sectors of international civil society as well as religious actors, the state and intergovernmental organisations (IGOs). Religious actors have gradually been able to enhance their skills and negotiation capacities not only in order to influence a number of development and climate policies,[15] but also to implement such policies in their communities through faith-based organisations' sustainable projects such as access to clean water and hygiene, reforestation and food security through agroforestry. The religious actors studied here are acquainted with different dimensions specific to development and more specifically sustainable development,

---

[13] Pierre-Yves Le Meur, "Le développement comme constructivisme. Point de vue anthropologique", *Sociétés politiques comparées, revue européenne d'analyse des sociétés politiques*, n°8, October 2008 www.fasopo.org, p. 3.

[14] Here "field" is to be understood in Bourdieu's sense which is central in his theory. The field is a relatively autonomous social microcosm formed with its own rules and challenges and within the macrocosm. For Bourdieu, fields (political, religious, artistic, etc.) are "networks of social relations, structured systems of social positions within which struggles take place over resources, stakes and access". Pierre Bourdieu, Loïc Wacquant, *Réponses. Pour une anthropologie réflexive*, Paris, Seuil, 1992.

[15] Duncan McDuie-Ra & John A. Rees, "Religious Actors, Civil Society and the Development Agenda: The Dynamics of Inclusion and Exclusion", *Journal of International Development*, 22, 2010, pp. 20–36.

which now represents a transversal and interdisciplinary research field that includes the central question of global warming.

In this study on climate change, the analysis of international political sociology that I favour here must take into account the cognitive dimension of the actors concerned, as well as their capacities in international relations. Some of them may have skills and, perhaps, experience of how international affairs work. In other words, they may have a long tradition of multi-track diplomacy[16] (see Chapter 4). Climate action is political and diplomatic in nature, because it can be effective in terms of mitigation only through states which implement sound environmental policies and legislations on a national scale. Therefore, we also have to understand the national context. This will be done through the case of South Africa and the nature of the local impact on the discourses and actions of transnational religious actors engaged in the cause of environmental protection and which remains essential in the study of their glocal[17] mobilisation. Climate action in the local context could be a consequence of the "boomerang effect",[18] meaning that foreign policy "comes home", but it is also part of the political will of national political stakeholders and the mobilisation of civil society to implement the climate agenda locally. Choosing South Africa as the case study is based on various factors in understanding local climate politics: it is a democratic country that can be considered as part of the Global South and has already hosted a Conference of the Parties—COP 17—of the UNFCCC; it is also a state that has an explicit public policy on the management of religious diversity and cooperates with religious actors within the framework of multi-level

[16] See among others, Joseph Montville, *The Arrow and the Olive Branch: A Case for Track Two Diplomacy*, Lexington, MA, Lexington Books, 1990; L. Diamond & J. McDonald, *Multi-track Diplomacy: A Systems Guide and Analysis*, Grinnell, Iowa, Iowa Peace Institute, 1994.

[17] Roland Robertson, «'Globalisation or Glocalisation?'», *The Journal of International Communication*, 1(1), 1994, pp. 33–52; Roland Robertson, *Globalization: Social Theory and Global Culture*, Londres, Sage, 1992. See also, Victor Roudometof: "The reality of internal globalization (or glocalization) is responsible for the transformation of people's everyday lives irrespective of whether they are transnational or not". Victor Roudometof, "Transnationalism, Cosmopolitanism and Glocalization", *Current Sociology*, 53 (1), 2005, p. 113.

[18] M. Keck & K. Sikkink, *Activists Beyond Borders*, Ithaca, Cornell University Press, 1998.

governance.[19] Therefore, the South African case will help us to understand the *process of the politicisation* of religious actors' mobilisation for climate mitigation and adaptation.

The perspective and methodology of international political sociology adopted here is based first of all on an analysis of the academic literature and international institutions' reports on the theme of religion and development, and of religion and climate change. Second, this perspective depends on a synthesis of the environmental and climate agreements adopted by the international community in order to frame the socio-historical context in which religious actors make their pronouncements on the issue of climate change. This context is nevertheless emphasised by religious actors themselves, whose actions in defence of the climate are conditioned by the position they have in the transnational climate field formed by their mobilisation for climate justice and sustainable development. After defining the context, it is then possible to better understand religious actors' stance in the transnational climate field formed by translocal networks,[20] based on several interviews and discourse analyses. Religious stakeholders seek above all to intervene on matters of inequality, climate injustice and the fight against poverty, all encompassed today under the broader term of sustainable development, which itself also has ethical foundations.[21] Since 2015, monitoring multilateral climate negotiations by following the reports on the United Nations Framework Convention on Climate Change (UNFCCC) website also made possible, among other things, a study of the press releases and other pronouncements of state representatives and religious actors during the Conferences of the Parties (COP) to the UNFCCC.

---

[19] Ian Bache & Matthew Flinders (eds.), *Multi-level Governance*, Oxford University Press, 2010.

[20] Peggy Levitt & Nina Glick Schiller, "Conceptualizing Simultaneity: A Transnational Social Field Perspective on Society", *The International Migration Review*, 38 (3), 2004, pp. 1002–1039.

[21] Marie-Claude Smouts, "Du patrimoine commun de l'humanité aux biens publics globaux", in Marie-Christine Cormier-Salem et al. (eds.), *Patrimoines naturels au Sud: Territoires, identités et stratégies locales* [online], Marseille, IRD Editions, 2005, pp. 53–70.

RELIGION AND STATE CLIMATE POLICIES

On the international scene, climate change remains first and foremost a matter for states to address through IGOs. States participate in the drafting of universal agreements for the preservation of the climate and commit themselves by legislative means to enforce the resulting rules in their respective countries. It is important to keep this theoretical and legislative principle in mind, even though civil society actors (NGOs, the youth, Indigenous People, women, faith-based organisations, individuals) as non-state international actors are increasingly concerned with the cause of climate change and are increasingly involved in collective mobilisation. The first milestones in responding to the challenge of global warming date back only to the 1990s with the first report of the Intergovernmental Panel on Climate Change (IPCC). The IPCC was created in 1988 by the World Meteorological Organization (WMO) and the United Nations Environment Programme (UNEP)[22]; its work led to the adoption of the Kyoto Protocol in 1997,[23] following several rounds of negotiations between states members of the UNFCC. Since then, the impact of civil society and religious institutions on the international scene has gained momentum. The latter are far from being peripheral protagonists in the action to protect the climate balance, since they represent a cosmopolitan force in the circulation of expertise on climate change. Moreover, religious actors as moral authorities exert a global ethical influence in the framework of multilateral negotiations on global warming and the environmental protection through the participation of religious leaders on these international platforms and their public calls for action.[24] Climate change has global impacts and is of paramount importance in terms of preserving common goods, collective security, justice and peace and waging the war on poverty, all of which are encompassed in the 17 Sustainable Development Goals (SDGs). The great challenge for all

---

[22] The main objective of the IPCC is to provide governments with scientific information necessary for their climate policies https://www.ipcc.ch/about/.

[23] R.K. Pachauri, "The IPCC: Establishing the Evidence", in Ernesto Zedillo (ed.), *Global Warming: Looking Beyond Kyoto*, Washington, DC, Brookings Institution Press, 2008, pp. 13–20.

[24] Robin Globus Veldman, Andrew Szasz, & Randolph Haluza-Delay, "Introduction: Climate Change and Religion—A Review of Existing Research", *Journal for the Study of Religion, Nature and Culture*, 6, November 2012, pp. 255–275; John Grim & Mary Evelyn Tucker, *Ecology and Religion*, Washington, DC, Island Press, 2014.

international actors, both religious and inter-state stakeholders involved in climate change, remains the imperative nature of their cooperation.[25] Indeed, as we have seen, only the state is in a position to bring multilateral climate negotiations to a successful conclusion in terms of legislative frameworks. Of course, and in accordance with a realist analysis of international relations, states' national interests are at the centre of their concerns.[26]

Climate action most often falls far short not only of the recommendations by scientific experts gathered in the IPCC, but also of the conclusions reached by the UN Conference on the Human Environment organised earlier in 1972. During the same year of 1972, the book *Limits to Growth*, issued by the Club of Rome, warned of the risk of an ecological resource crisis in the twenty-first century. The matter of risk awareness is at the centre of a climate analysis, as Ulrich Beck[27] had argued in 1986 already in his work on the risk society. Effective governance and the construction of a safe world for present and future generations therefore require a high level of awareness, conscience and even a moral basis, as is repeatedly emphasised by, among others, religious actors and not only in the warnings about anthropogenic dangers in expert reports.

However, one can legitimately ask about the nature of religious actors' actions in support of mitigating climate change: is there a possibility of influencing political decision-makers? Do they participate in international public actions and policies in favour of protecting the climate? In order to answer these questions regarding religious actors and their actions, it is advisable in sociology of international relations, first of all, not to confuse the secularisation of political institutions with the secularisation of populations. In France, for example, secularism must be understood in the first place as a public policy that embodies a political and institutional historical process specific to the country. Since the state remains a major player in the climate enterprise, should international relations here be understood from the exclusive perspective of secular institutions? The international public policies implemented by states are primarily aimed at

[25] Bettina Laville, Stéphanie Thiebault, & Agathe Euzen, *Quelles solutions face au changement climatique ?*, Paris, CNRS Publications, 2015.

[26] Hans J. Morgenthau & K.W. Thompson, *Politics Among Nations: The Struggle for Power and Peace*, 6th ed., Knopf, 1985.

[27] Ulrich, Beck, *Risk Society: Towards a New Modernity*, London, Sage Publications, 1992.

populations who on the whole uphold religious practices or beliefs on the international scene.[28] This is one reason why the recognition of religious identity and denominational organisations in the field of development has gradually become an international standard. Multilateral organisations on climate change will grant civil society as well as religious stakeholders a participative role to play within international forums. The challenge here is to understand the nature of religious actors' action and discourse. These two dimensions influence each other and can be understood together as a new form of religious transnationalism for taking action on climate change.

[28] According to a 2012 study by the Pew Research Centre, 84% of the world population has a religious affiliation. https://www.pewforum.org/2018/06/13/how-religious-com mitment-varies-by-country-among-people-of-all-ages/.

CHAPTER 2

Cosmopolitanism in Globalisation and New Forms of Transnational Religious Mobilisation

Cosmopolitan practices are mostly related to non-state actors' transnational mobilisation. I will not go back to the debate about "methodological nationalism" in order to understand the importance of transnational modes of action in our contemporary world. "Methodological cosmopolitanism", coined by Ulrich Beck,[1] is associated in this analysis of religious transnationalism in particular with the notion of relations to the Other. However, we also need to investigate the context which enables, but at the same time also constrains, the discourses and actions of confessional actors who promote cosmopolitanism. This context will be analysed mostly in the current stage of multilateralism directed towards international development since the end of the Cold War and which influences new processes of globalisation and transnationalisation.

Non-State Actors and Changes in World Politics

In the 1990s, after the collapse of the bipolar international system, one-third of the world's population was still experiencing dire poverty. The post-Cold War international community saw the need to organise a global

---

[1] U. Beck, *Cosmopolitan Vision*, Cambridge, Polity Press, 2006.

© The Author(s), under exclusive license to Springer Nature Switzerland AG 2022
S. Sadouni, *Religious Transnationalism and Climate Change*, Human Rights Interventions,
https://doi.org/10.1007/978-3-031-10610-1_2

11

programme for poverty alleviation, which would in turn boost sustainable development. The Millennium Development Goals were adopted in 2000 by the General Assembly of the United Nations for a period of 15 years. A new international agenda, Agenda 2030 for Sustainable Development, was launched in 2015, the same year as the adoption of the Paris Agreement.

If religious actors have focused on the issue of climate change and made it a priority in their actions, it is because of the poor who are most vulnerable to—and therefore the first victims of—climate change. Because of their social teaching and ethical position on poverty, religious actors have the capacity to participate in the implementation of the Paris Agreement, which stipulates: "this Agreement, in enhancing the implementation of the Convention, including its objective, aims to strengthen the global response to the threat of climate change, in the context of sustainable development and efforts to eradicate poverty" (Paris Agreement, Article 2). Although the universal objective of protecting the planet has priority, protection of the poor and the most vulnerable is central in the discourse and actions of religious actors. All religions share this concern for the poor, and this will lead them to conduct similar actions for climate justice. First, let's look at the level of poverty in the world and the measures which have been taken by the international community to alleviate poverty.

One of the most important tools to advance global development, namely the UN's Millennium Development Goals, had as their objective the reduction of poverty by 2015. The results were convincing. Indeed, there was a noticeable drop in poverty in the Global South from 31 to 20% between 1997 and 2007. For example, China's rate dropped by nearly half from 33 to 14%, which is an important improvement compared to poverty rates in Africa, which has continued to suffer high levels of poverty (50%). The World Bank states that between 1990 and 2008 incomes per person in the Global South rose from about $3,000 to $5,500. In the Global North, the respective figures were a rise from about $20,000 to $31,000. The inequality remains, even though social progress can be observed in the Global South without, however, reaching the higher levels of the Global North.[2] The number of people living in extreme poverty was 736 million in 2015, compared to nearly 2

---

[2] Joshua S. Goldstein & Jon C. Pevehouse, *International Relations*, Boston, Pearson, 2013, pp. 425–426.

billion in 1990, representing nearly 35% of the world population in 1990, compared to 10% in 2015. These figures are high, especially when we think about the international situation after the fall of the Berlin Wall and the beginnings of a new international system based on unipolar American power. Between 1990 and 2015, the number of people living in extreme poverty was reduced by over a billion. We can ask whether these figures are the consequence of an international system that has moved gradually from a bipolar system to a multilateral system ?

It was estimated that in 2020, approximately 700 million people would be living in extreme poverty (international poverty line: $1.90/day), i.e. they would not have access to basic food and health care. These populations are concentrated mainly in Africa, where income levels have been among the lowest in the world for decades.[3] However, the consequences of the COVID-19 pandemic have slowed down this trend of shrinking world poverty. It was estimated that between 88 and 115 million, more people would be living in poverty in 2020. The issue of global access to vaccination against COVID-19 reveals again the efficiency of a multilateral international system that could promote interdependence, solidarity and state cooperation.

Analysing the process of globalisation implies looking not only at the different flows (economic, financial, cultural, migratory, among others) facilitated by the rise of modern technologies and communication, but also at the supra-territorial organisations[4] such as the United Nations' system linking individuals and nations by focusing on two main objectives: peace and security. Hence globalisation can be considered as the circumstance that could favour the development of a new ethic of being in an international context. This is illustrated by the term "cosmopolitanism".[5] The objective of ending poverty, also considered as a matter of security and social peace, has unified religious aspirations for the kind of globalisation that can promote shared wealth and greater social justice. In

---

[3] https://openknowledge.worldbank.org/bitstream/handle/10986/30418/211330 ovFR.pdf?sequence=35&isAllowed=y (page 2). https://blogs.worldbank.org/fr/ope ndata/l-extreme-pauvrete-continue-de-progresser-en-afrique-subsaharienne

[4] J. A. Scholte, *Globalization: A Critical Introduction*, Londres, Macmillan, 2000, p. 40.

[5] According to Jan N. Pieterse, "*Nowadays Globalization Is the Circumstance and Cosmopolitanism Is the Ethos*"; Jan Nederveen Pieterse, "Emancipatory Cosmopolitanism: Towards an Agenda", *Development and Change*, 37 (6), 2006, pp. 1247–1257.

the field of climate action, the international role of religious actors—faith-based NGO representatives and churches—is therefore undeniable. The latter are non-state actors whose influence in international relations, hitherto neglected, is beginning to be the subject of scientific studies.[6] They also demonstrate not only the different dimensions of the circulation of religion, but also the multifaceted character of identity and belonging in our globalised world. Political scientists and international relations scholars have long ignored the role of religions in contemporary international politics. This epistemological and methodological position can be attributed to the influence of secularisation theses linked to Enlightenment hypotheses that saw "disenchantment" with the world illustrated by the disavowal of religion from individuals' public and private lives in the Western world, for example. The post-Cold War period, marked by the fall of the bipolar international system, on the other hand, has seen the emergence of culturalist theories of international relations such as those developed by Samuel Huntington in his "clash of civilisations".[7] When, by the end of the 1990s, religion was taken into consideration in international analysis at all, it was from the perspective of attributing to it the power to represent ideological forces that could lead either to conflict or to strengthening world peace. This essentialist approach to religion has subsequently given way to a functionalist approach to religion in international development (see Chapter 3).

TRANSNATIONAL SOCIAL FIELD

In this study, the neo-Weberian approach to religion in international relations[8] involves identifying stakeholders, religious actors *per se*, and

[6] Timothy Samuel Shah, Alfred Stepan, & Monica Duffy Toft, *Rethinking Religion and World Affairs*, New York, Open University Press, 2012; Elizabeth Shakman Hurd, *The Politics of Secularism in International Relations*, Princeton, Princeton University Press, 2008.

[7] Samuel P. Huntington, "The Clash of Civilizations?", *Foreign Affairs*, 72 (3), 1993, pp. 22–49; S. Huntington, *The Clash of Civilizations and the Remaking of World Order*, Simon & Schuster, 1996. For a critical analysis of culturalist theories on religion and Islam especially, see among other, J.-L Esposito, *The Islamic threat: Myth or Reality?*, New York, Oxford University Press, 1999.

[8] Cecelia Lynch, "A Neo-Weberian Approach to Religion in International Relations", *International Theory*, 1 (3), 2009, pp. 381–408; T. B. Schwarz & C. Lynch, *Religion in International Relations*, Oxford Research Encyclopedia of Politics, 2016.

understanding the meaning they ascribe to their international actions on a multilateral international platform such as the Conferences of the Parties of the UNFCCC. We need to study how these actors conduct a multidimensional relationship with other actors, both state and non-state, and illustrated by cosmopolitan practices. Furthermore, the transnational perspective adopted here will enrich the international political sociology of international relations which aims to understand the complex, cross-border relationships that religious players maintain and how they negotiate them in a context marked by specific historical, political, economic and geographical factors.[9] In its interdisciplinary approach, international political sociology furthermore takes into account interdependencies and their historicity in the study of interactions,[10] which will serve to better understand religious actors' climate change programme.

Therefore, this study aims to explore another perspective on the globalisation of the religious dimension. Proceeding from the concept of cosmopolitanism, this work intends to analyse confessional actors—mainly Muslims and Christians—endowed with transnational capacities in a situation of interreligious relations that have an impact on the international scene, as well as, for some, on international politics. Indeed, religious actors' practices in international relations are marked by a cosmopolitan approach, that is, through their openness to the Other and their projection into a transnational space, they can have an impact on the local and vice versa. It is therefore appropriate to look at the nature of the "locality"[11] or "glocality", which is produced by various transnational social fields (see Chapter 5). This relationship to the Other, although constructed differently in each instance, can be identified for the religious actors studied here and constitutes the basis of their discourses and positions. The final objective here is to approach a critical analysis of the "ethos of cosmopolitanism" in the context of globalisation—in short, a political sociology of cosmopolitanism in international relations.

---

[9] F. Kratochwil, "Religion and (Inter-)national Politics: On the Heuristics of Identities, Structures, and Agents", *Alternatives*, 30 (2), 2005, pp. 113–140.

[10] This requires us to think about international relations in the light of different theoretical currents in international relations (constructivism and critical theories, for example) and different disciplines in the humanities, including political philosophy.

[11] Arjun Appadurai, "The Production of Locality", in R. Fardon (ed.), *Counterworks: Managing the Diversity of Knowledge*, London, Routledge, 1995, pp. 204–225.

Why choose the term "cosmopolitan" or "cosmopolitanism" in an analysis of religious transnationalism in the field of climate change? Cosmopolitanism, a concept used by transnational theory for the study of identity and relations of otherness,[12] will give the whole of this work its coherence. Cosmopolitanism is a heuristic concept, because it enables us to identify not only the nature of the public actions carried out by religious actors, but also to understand the ways in which they present the issue of the relationship between poverty, inequalities, social justice and the governance of the climate crisis. The question now is how we can understand international relations through examining the mutual relations between politics, religion and society. "Religion and politics", on the one hand, and "religion and society", on the other, are related to what Ulrich Beck calls "the sociology of the second age of modernity"[13] and will be studied through a transnational perspective and the concept of cosmopolitanism.[14] Beck in fact takes the view that society and its cosmopolitisation is the product of new social and political mutations that cannot be understood within the strict nation-state framework, since solidarity, social cohesion—notions which Durkheim scrutinised— are increasingly articulated around transnational networks. Therefore, the notion of "the international" needs to be clarified as a *transnational social field* and characterised by the entanglement of the internal and the external. Indeed, the analysis of transnational activities in international political sociology, conceptualised in terms of transnational social fields, also looks, as we have seen, at the local context, the society of the emergence and/or reception of transnational mobilisation. The premise of my book is that transnational and cosmopolitical relations are mutually influential and increasingly based on the creation of a shared space for the reinvention and promotion of common values, responsibilities and actions for climate mitigation, and for adaptations that transcend

---

[12] S. Khagram & P. Levitt (eds.), *The Transnational Studies Reader. Intersections & Innovations*, New York, Routledge, 2008.

[13] Ulrich Beck, "The Cosmopolitan Perspective: Sociology of the Second Age of Modernity", in S. Khagram & P. Levitt (eds.), *The Transnational Studies Reader* ..., op. cit., pp. 222–230.

[14] In her book "Artifacts and Allegiances. How Museums put the Nation and the World on display", Peggy Levitt suggests museums might play a part in creating a cosmopolitan citizen. P. Levitt, *Artifacts and Allegiances. How Museums put the Nation and the World on Display*, Oakland, University of California Press, 2015.

national borders, social polarisations and divisions. This will be illustrated with reference to the religious actors' discourses and actions during the Conference of the Parties of the UNFCCC but also in local settings.

The work on climate change by faith-based NGOs in post-1994 South Africa, for example, is linked simultaneously to the theme of "religion and society" and "religion and politics". The analysis of the cosmopolitisation of society entails a closer look at the local context, the nation-state (in this case South Africa), from the perspective of methodological nationalism, which is otherwise decried by some authors of cosmopolitanism such as Beck. Environmental NGOs, such as SAFCEI (Southern African Faith Communities Environment Institute), describe a trajectory of activist organisations participating in the formation of a multi-faith social movement in the local space that advocates the protection of the planet. Regarding the dimension of religion and politics, the study of non-state and religious actors on the international scene and locally shows us how political change can be thought of in conjunction with religious change. This will also be illustrated with the case of SAFCEI, which is also committed to a critical relationship with the South African government and to debate on democracy. Consequently, it is advisable to adopt a new approach to international relations that no longer see the religious to the political as opposed on the local and global level, as this risks a failure to understand the turning points observed in the international arena.

In a neo-Weberian and interdisciplinary perspective, we not only need to analyse the meaning given by religious actors to international action but also to their strategies. These religious actors influence the mutations of politics and religion by negotiating power relations with other international actors, states or IGOs, in a specific transnational social field. An example of this is Muslim organisations such as the UK-based Islamic Foundation for Ecology and Environmental Sciences (IFEES) involved in the Faith for Earth Initiative of the United Nations Environment Programme (UNEP), which in 2020 launched the project *Mizan*, Arabic for "balance", a future charter "designed to showcase Islam's teachings on the environment and spur the world's 1.8 billion Muslims to embrace sustainability as part of their everyday lives".[15] Individuals and Islamic institutions that cannot steer this ambitious programme of socio-economic and religious changes on their own are brought together in

---

[15] https://www.unep.org/es/node/28601.

order to deal with the climate change crisis, among other things. The analysis of this specific transnational social field will consist not only of studying the practices that do not necessarily condition cross-border mobility,[16] nor the force and power relationships that can be deployed there.[17] All confessional actors studied here deploy translocal activities and discourses that are important in the analysis of the international relations composed of state and non-state actors, including religious institutions, NGOs and intergovernmental organisations (IGOs).

Highlighting a constructivist sociology of international relations,[18] still a dimension of the research programme of international political sociology, reveals the importance of both the context and the co-constitution of identities and interests (the ideational and material dimensions) that can inform religious actors' meaning and strategies. International relations must be analysed in terms of the social interplay of actors and the dialectic between the local and the global, especially for the study of transnational field of climate action which are the sites *par excellence* where the local and the global intersect. Moreover, it is not only a matter of analysing the glocalisation/translocalisation of the religious, but also its official internationalisation, i.e. its integration into and participation in intergovernmental organisations and forums (see Chapter 4).

Studying the religious actors in the field of climate action will make it possible to understand not only international relations in their multilateral

[16] For Nina Glick Schiller: "The actors in a transnational social field are *not necessarily* migrants or mobile individuals (…). The concept draws attention to the processes that develop and maintain networks of social relations across borders as part of the everyday life of the members of the network". N. Glick Schiller, "The Transnational Migration Paradigm: Global Perspectives on Migration Research", in D. Halm & Z. Sezgin (eds.), *Migration and Organized Civil Society*, London, Routledge, 2013 p. 26; See also Peggy Levitt and Nina Glick Schiller, "Conceptualizing Simultaneity: A Transnational Social Field Perspective on Society", *The International Migration Review*, 38 (3), 2004, pp. 1002–1039. In the same way, the authors stress the importance of simultaneity: "Simultaneity, or living lives that incorporate daily activities, routines, and institutions located both in a destination country and transnationally, is a possibility that needs to be theorized and explored", p. 1003.

[17] N. Glick Schiller, "Transnational Social Fields and Imperialism: Bringing a Theory of Power to Transnational Studies", *Anthropological Theory*, 5 (4), 2005, pp. 439–461; V. Roudometof, "Transnationalism, Cosmopolitanism, and Glocalization"; P. Bourdieu, «Genèse et structure du champ religieux», *Revue française de sociologie*, 12 (3), juillet-septembre 1971, pp. 295–334.

[18] F. Kratochwil, "Religion and (Inter-)national Politics: On the Heuristics of Identities, Structures, and Agents", *Alternatives*, 30 (2), 2005, pp. 113–140.

forms and non-state dimensions, but also the influence of globalisation on the modes of subjectivation and transnational collective action for climate mitigation and development (discussed in Chapters 3 and 4). Globalisation as a social process therefore also influences community formation as well as individual biographies, as will be seen with SAFCEI (see Chapter 5).

Cosmopolitical Practices in International Relations

Cosmopolitanism has a positive connotation in the everyday language of most languages. It is also used to describe the homogenising commercial globalisation of the twenty-first century through, for example, the hotel chains that offer a globalised service and that are found all over the world. It is seen as a manifestation of the upper- and middle-class mentality arising from globalisation.[19] Cosmopolitanism most often evokes an ethical stance or the philosophical ideal of "world citizenship". However, Beck claims that the concept of cosmopolitanism as applied to the analysis of international relations must be distinguished from the philosophical approach. Here, it is to be understood not in its Kantian sense[20] (a form of belonging to the world that transcends other forms of allegiance), but in a simpler analytical sense. In concrete terms, it is a matter of taking note of the extent of transnational phenomena, but also of the plurality of actors who intend to take part in world affairs without losing sight of their multiple identities in relation to the Other: NGOs and other representatives of civil society, not forgetting states themselves.[21] The latter remain important actors in international relations, in contemporary society and in the transnational climate field studied in this volume.

Cosmopolitan practices must thus be understood in international relations as social facts. In particular, Beck contends that "*banal cosmopolitanism* is manifested in concrete, everyday ways by the fact that differentiations between us and them are becoming confused, both at the national and at international level".[22] What is important to remember about the

---

[19] Mike Featherstone, "Cosmopolis: An Introduction", *Theory, Culture, and Society*, 19 (1–2), 2002, pp. 1–16.

[20] Kant believed cosmopolitism guaranteed "permanent peace".

[21] David Held, *Democracy and the Global Order: From the Modern State to Cosmopolitan Governance*, Stanford, CA, Stanford University Press, 1995.

[22] U. Beck, *Cosmopolitan Vision*, Cambridge, Polity Press, 2006, p. 10.

notion of cosmopolitanism in the analysis of religious actors in international relations and their actions in the field of climate change is the way cosmopolitan practices affect the relationship they can have to the world and to the Other.[23] The aim is not to contribute to a normative and philosophical discourse on cosmopolitanism, or to determine its positive or negative aspects,[24] but rather to identify its political, cultural and social roots and impact. It is all about approaching cosmopolitanism as a form of practice,[25] not as an idea about harmony among peoples or a proposal for making the world a better place. The concept of cosmopolitanism is a tool for understanding the internal–external relations of faith-based actors and their relationship to the Other in the specific *transnational field of climate change*.

From a transnational studies perspective, using the term cosmopolitanism helps to develop a glocal analysis of the religious dimension and its interfaith component; it is not a matter here of "confusing globalization and cosmopolitanism".[26] After working with the notion of cosmopolitanism, I confirmed its usefulness, because the terms "global" and "globalisation" alone did not convey the meaning of the religious actors' practices observed in international relations and particularly in the domain of climate change. The relationship to the Other was often highlighted in the interviews conducted with religious actors and in their speeches; this translated into a new form of transnational religious mobilisation or "religious modernity" that they expressed in similar ways. Moreover, studying international relations also means addressing, from an epistemological point of view, the claim made by the liberal school of international relations for the desirability for societies and institutions to reduce ignorance of the Other, which often leads to marginalisation, rejection and sometimes conflict with the Other. According to the liberal

[23] Muriel Rouyer, Catherine de Wrangel, Emmanuelle Bousquet and Stefania Cubeddu (eds.), *Regards sur le cosmopolitisme européen - Frontières et identités*, Brussels, Peter Lang, 2011; Vincenzo Cicchelli & G. Truc (eds.), "De la mondialisation au cosmopolitisme", *Problèmes politiques et sociaux*, n° 986–987, July–August 2011.

[24] Anthony Appiah, Kwame, *Cosmopolitanism: Ethics in a World of Strangers*, New York, W. W. Norton, 2006.

[25] Michel Certeau (de), *L'invention du quotidien. 1-Arts de faire*, Paris, Gallimard, 1990.

[26] Vincenzo Cicchelli, Sylvie Octobre, "Pour une approche cosmopolite de la globalization",*Sociétés Plurielles*, Presses de l'INALCO, 2018, Épistémologies du pluriel (hal-01692718), p. 3. See also Pieterse (2006).

school of international relations, while it is considered good for people to live in peace, it is also good from a humanist point of view for international institutions to establish dialogue, cooperation and a partnership between them in a spirit of mutual recognition.[27]

"Cosmopolitanism" and "cosmopolitisation", terms used by Beck,[28] relate to the "internal globalisation" of national societies. However, this study will also reveal the epistemological limits of what Beck[29] suggests in using the terminology of "methodological nationalism"; this will not be a matter of "throwing the baby out with the bathwater", because the dominant method in the social sciences at present entails studying contemporary social facts in the light of the international relations of states, especially when it comes to the eminently translocal and global issue of climate change. The link between the internal and the external is central to transnational analysis and, of course, to international political sociology. Therefore, dialogue with religious actors participating in international civil society becomes an international norm of cooperation for IGOs and states. This can be considered as an aspect of the Sustainable Development Goals. States' national interest in the transnational field of climate protection is increasingly based on renunciation of competition in favour of intergovernmental cooperation as well as cooperation with non-state actors, even at the cost sometimes of losing part of a state's own sovereignty.

Cosmopolitan practices in turn also entail an ethical capacity to participate in the formation of international norms of religious tolerance and dialogue. We can observe this in the UN's institutions. For example, the dialogue of religions was inaugurated by the World Interfaith Harmony Week aimed to promote a culture of peace and non-violence. Since the General Assembly's resolution of 2010, World Interfaith Harmony Week has become an annual event observed during the first week of

---

[27] Thomas Lindemann and Julie Saada, «Théories de la reconnaissance dans les relations internationales», *Cultures & Conflits*, 87, 2012, 7–25; P. Hayden & K. Schick (eds.), *Recognition and Global Politics. Critical Encounters Between State and World*, Manchester University Press, 2016.

[28] Ulrich Beck, "The Cosmopolitan Society and its Enemies", *Theory, Culture and Society*, 19 (1–2), 2002, pp. 17–44; U. Beck, "The Cosmopolitan Perspective: Sociology of the Second Age of Modernity", *British Journal of Sociology*, 51 (1), 2008, pp. 79–105.

[29] U. Beck, *Cosmopolitan Vision*, Cambridge, Polity Press, 2006.

February. This resolution institutionalised interfaith dialogue as an important dimension of a culture of peace promotion within the UN system and therefore encourages all states to convey the message to recognise "the imperative need for dialogue among different faiths and religions to enhance mutual understanding, harmony and cooperation among people". In 2021, the UN pursued this initiative and inaugurated the International Day of Human Fraternity on 4 February.[30]

As far as the religious cosmopolitanism embodied by the actors studied is concerned, this will be analysed along a spectrum describing different forms of cosmopolitan thought and practice. This social reality must be measured by distinguishing three categories of cosmopolitan practices:

–the nature and degree of interactions with the Other as embodied in inter-religious dialogue[31];

- the nature and degree of transnational mobility: the conduct of and participation in international conferences, the circulation of discourse via the internet and through the literature, the creation of transnational organisations constituting a partisan apparatus;
- the nature of the political attachment to a particular territory, since the intertwining of the internal and the external is at the heart of the phenomenon of religious cosmopolitanism.[32]

Religious actors position themselves differently along this spectrum and through their discourses and activities demonstrate the use of more or less powerful and influential international capacities within the transnational field of climate change.

What we can observe so far is a "re-enchantment" of reality in the very broad field of sustainable development, including climate change. Work on the influence of religions in global affairs emphasises in particular that the initiative for cooperation between international organisations and faith-based actors lies first with international institutions and then

---

[30] https://www.un.org/en/observances/interfaith-harmony-week.

[31] J. Fahy & J. Haynes (eds.), Special issue "Interfaith on the World Stage", *The Review of Faith & International Affairs*, 16, 2018.

[32] As underlined by Victor Roudometof: «(…) attachment to locality is consequential in terms of openness towards outsiders» (Roudometof 2005: 124).

with individual internationalists, who can be both academics and international experts. All of them have initiated exchanges with faith-based actors in order to understand the influence and role of religions in international public policies for development (see Chapter 3). Over the past five years, we have observed that interfaith climate action illustrates how a strictly secularised reading of international development, understood in the common sense as strictly state-oriented and non-religious, precludes an appreciation of the impact on the local and international scene of the decisions and actions led by religious actors. The UNEP's executive office, which launched the Faith for Earth Strategic Engagement, aims, for example, to bring together faith actors for action in emergencies and in the field of sustainable development, calling "on everyone—countries, cities, the private sector, individuals, and faith-based organizations—to strengthen their actions to mitigate climate change, restore ecosystems, and protect the health of the planet without delay".[33] Concerted action and cooperation are considered as urgent in addressing climate change, which became a top priority on the international policy agenda. A multi-level governance system is therefore illustrated today by, among others, governmental structures and decisions, transnational networks and international institutions all acting together for the mitigation of climate change. Religious cosmopolitan practices represent a dimension of multi-level governance, bottom-up initiatives led by non-state religious actors.[34]

---

[33] These are the words of Iyad Abumoghli, Director of Faith for Earth Strategic Engagement with Faith-based Organizations Executive Office United Nations Environment Programme Nairobi, Kenya. In United Nations Environment Programme and Parliament of the World's Religions (2020), *Faith for Earth: A Call for Action*, UNEP, Nairobi. https://wedocs.unep.org/bitstream/handle/20.500.11822/33991/FECA.pdf? sequence=1&isAllowed=y.

[34] According to Rolf Lidskog and Ingemar Elander, "there are basically two types of multi-level governance (...). The federal and the regime models of environmental governance are expressions of the first type, whereas the cosmopolitan model is of the latter kind, as illustrated by World Social Forum and similar bottom-up initiatives". (....) "Thus, roughly speaking, we have two parallel sets of institutions, one formal, going from global agreements derived from the Kyoto Protocol via EU and national governments down to local governments, and another, informal one of a much looser kind, linking social movements, voluntary associations, single-issue pressure groups, private businesses, research institutions and sometimes also local governments to each other". Rolf Lidskog & Ingemar Elander, "Addressing Climate Change Democratically. Multi-Level Governance, Transnational Networks and Governmental Structures", *Sustainable Development*, 18, 2010, p. 38.

Religious cosmopolitanism and global warming must be understood, first of all, as a spectrum/continuum—a model I borrow from the physical sciences—of cosmopolitical traits that confessional actors adopt according to the context of their actions, their discourses and within a transnational field of climate activism. Religious cosmopolitanism is heterogeneous and can be studied through the transnational trajectories of official churches and representatives of faith-based NGOs. Religious actors, in cooperation with their communities and congregations, international organisations and states, therefore participate through their speeches and actions in the construction of a field of transnational climate activism that also embodies power relations. This will be further highlighted in the examination of the climate-oriented actions of religious actors within the framework of multilateral negotiations (Chapter 4) and the space of the South African nation-state (Chapter 5).

The international political sociology of cosmopolitan practices embodied in different categories of religious actors (churches, NGOs) in international relations, and especially in the field of climate change, will therefore illuminate new modes of religious transnationalism based on deliberation and participation within multilateral platform. This is not a case of generalising the conclusions of this study to apply to all religious actors. Even if we live in an increasingly globalised world, not all individuals or all religious actors adopt cosmopolitical practices that address a relationship with the Other and engage in transnational mobilisation within multilateral forums for the protection of the environment, the future of humanity and the planet.

CHAPTER 3

Religions from the Field of Development to Climate Change

Scientific interest in issues related to the relationship between development and religion is recent. Specifically, little work seems to have been published on the subject of religion and sustainable development goals. According to the economist Jeffrey Sachs, the notion of sustainable development in a well-functioning society can only be formulated on the basis of four objectives: economic prosperity, social inclusion and cohesion, environmental sustainability and good governance by key social actors, including governments and businesses.[1] The religious actors studied here have adopted a stance on the issues of environmental protection, biodiversity, social cohesion and governance. Even though the official media have not relayed their statements widely—this includes comments made by Pope Francis, who is the head of the Catholic Church and one of the most emblematic religious actors and head of a state, the Vatican City—they are present on other media platforms such as YouTube, among others.

The exclusively secularist stance of the social sciences would therefore not have helped to understand changes in the religious sphere, especially

---

[1] J. Sachs pursues this by emphasising on the difficulties ahead: "Yet the stakes are high. Achieving sustainable development on our crowded, unequal, and degraded planet is the most important challenge facing our generation". Jeffrey D. Sachs, *The Age of Sustainable Development*, New York, Columbia University Press, 2015, p. 4.

S. Sadouni, *Religious Transnationalism and Climate Change*, Human Rights Interventions, https://doi.org/10.1007/978-3-031-10610-1_3

its influence on (international) development. However, religions and religious impulses have always played an essential role in humanitarian actions and more particularly and paradoxically during colonial times. The religious arm of colonisation contributed to the rise of humanitarianism[2] and to regarding individuals in need of development as inferior to the white Christian man. It's worth remembering that when one speaks of development,[3] the point of departure is a comparison in order to measure development against the position of the Other, who is most often deemed underdeveloped. In other words, religion instrumentalised for colonial political purposes was partly conducive to the emergence of the field of international development. The question is: Why was religion ignored for so long in the analysis of development during the period after the Second World War, which was also the period of decolonisation? When looking at international post-war development, it is necessary to integrate into this reflexive social science analysis the central role played by the realist theory in the discipline of international relations. This current emerged essentially in the aftermath of the Second World War, marking a new international system embodied in, among other things, the creation of the United Nations. The state-centric approach focused on the power relations between states that were regarded as exclusively constituting the international system and it therefore ignored the complexity of world politics. The concept of power alone is not able to explain diverse outcomes (for example, victory in conflicts, global reputation and influence) as military and economic resources are not the only capabilities wielded by states. More and more, NGOs were gaining a high status, communicating globally, while transnational companies became important actors of economic and political change in global politics by controlling economic resources.[4] The secularisation theories that dominate social science themes are not the only factors responsible for positing religion as a marginal actor, since realism in international relations has consistently ignored the role of non-state actors in power politics on the international

---

[2] M. Barnett, *Empire of Humanity: A History of Humanitarianism*, New York, Cornell University Press, 2011.

[3] The issue of sustainable development that emerged in the 1980s has a completely different meaning (I will get back to this later).

[4] P. Willetts, *Non-Governmental Organizations in World Politics. The Construction of Global Governance*, London, Routledge, 2010.

scene.[5] This particular aspect of the theory of realism has not been sufficiently taken into account in the scientific literature on the relationship
between religion and development.[6]

However, since the 2000s there has been an about-turn in the situation with the publication of numerous articles and books on religion
and development, which has since become a "fashionable" topic.[7] This
"religious turnaround" in development studies began, according to the
academic literature, with the actions of international organisations, particularly the World Bank. Indeed, the creation in 1998 of a platform for
dialogue, namely Development Dialogue on Values and Ethics, was one
of the first significant initiatives by James Wolfensohn, then World Bank
President, and George Carey, Anglican Archbishop of Canterbury at the
time. The national and international dialogue between religious actors
and international development organisations was intended to contribute
to fighting the high levels of poverty, as indicated in Chapter 2, and later
led to the creation of the World Faith Development Dialogue (WFDD).[8]
Other initiatives led by NGOs, governmental ministries and international organisations continued the weak momentum initiated by the
World Bank. Universities then took up this research theme.[9] However,

[5] Robert Cox, as an international relations critical theorist, put forward this formula, the
most frequently cited in his work: "Theory is always for someone and for some purpose".
Robert Cox, *Production, Power, and World Order: Social Forces in the Making of History*,
New York, Columbia University Press, 1987.

[6] Indeed, this can be highlighted by reading Jeffrey Haynes's work. See in particular
John Fahy & Jeffrey Haynes, "Introduction: Interfaith on the World Stage", *The Review
of Faith & International Affairs*, 16 (3), 2018, pp. 1–8.

[7] Ben Jones & Marie Juul Petersen, "Instrumental, Narrow, Normative? Reviewing
Recent Work on Religion and Development", *Third World Quarterly*, 32 (7), 2011,
p. 1292.

[8] WFDD was coordinated by Katherine Marshall. She had an advisory position with
the World Bank and developed the WFDD within the Georgetown University Research
Center, the *Berkley Center for Religion, Peace and World Affairs*. She has also co-edited
several volumes on religion and development. Katherine Marshall & L. Keough, *Mind,
Heart and Soul in the Fight Against Poverty*, Washington, DC, World Bank, 2004;
Katherine Marshall & L. Keough, *Finding Global Balance: Common Ground Between the
Worlds of Development and Faith*, Washington, DC, World Bank, 2005; K. Marshall & R.
Marsh, *Millennium Challenges for Development and Faith Institutions*, Washington, DC,
World Bank, 2003; K. Marshall & M. Van Saanen, *Development and Faith: Where Mind,
Heart, and Soul Work Together*, Washington, DC, World Bank, 2007.

[9] See, among others, Jeffrey Haynes, *Religion and Development: Conflict or Cooperation?*, Basingstoke, Palgrave Macmillan, 2007; Gerrie Ter Haar (ed.), *Religion and*

the production of academic literature has suffered from a functionalist approach to religion mainly because of an epistemological stance influenced by public administrations and international organisations. They were the first to initiate an inquiry into the potential and role of religions in international development.[10] Once again, it is worth considering the role of the state in order to understand the functionalism of these studies, reports and scientific productions. International organisations, which are by definition intergovernmental organisations (IGOs), will make their decisions in accordance with the objectives indicated by states and their representatives. The state may give preference to the non-state partners it considers capable of cooperating in international public policies implemented by sovereign states. It seems that the dominant analysis used adopts a functionalist rather than a constructivist approach as a matter of course. Experts have therefore found it difficult to construct a field of knowledge independent from organisational expectations in order to assess the impact of religions in achieving national and international development goals.[11]

Beyond endogenous factors, the religious policies of international organisations such as the World Bank, the UN and the foreign ministries of major powers such as the United States are also contributing to the emergence of an internationalisation of religious actors similar to that experienced by other religious actors such as Desmond Tutu in South Africa during the struggle against apartheid.[12] Indeed, academics were aware of the growing role of foreign diplomacy and international organisations in denouncing the apartheid regime in the 1980s, but also more

---

Development: Ways of Transforming the World, New York, Columbia University Press, 2011.

[10] (Ben Jones and Marie Juul Petersen 2011).

[11] See more particularly a critical analysis of academic research as well Katherine Marshall's work on the functionalist approach to religions and the dichotomy that developed between the religious and the secular: Philip Fountain, "The Myth of Religious NGOs: Development Studies and the Return of Religion", in Gilles Carbonnier, *Religion and Development*, Geneva, Graduate Institute Publications/Palgrave Macmillan, 2013, pp. 9–30.

[12] A. Klotz, *Norms in International Relations: The Struggle Against Apartheid*, Ithaca, Cornell University Press, 1995.

generally in the institutionalisation of post-conflict techniques and hybrid peace-building models.[13]

Intergovernmental organisations (IGO) recognise that faiths have the ability to sensitise their religious communities and their influence in the public space is a guarantee of their participation in the international community. Through their speeches and actions, IGOs in favour of a mobilisation of civil society participate in the construction of a so-called liberal international order based more and more on the cooperation of state and religious actors, without confusing their respective prerogatives. Liberal ideas here are essentially based on the construction and circulation of international standards, including human rights, religious tolerance and the fight against poverty and inequalities—inequalities that religious actors wish to eradicate, as will be seen in the case of the striving for climate justice. As for IGOs, secularism in the international context implies a recognition of all religious actors and the possibility of offering them all an equal role as interlocutors. They now consider religious actors as key players in international environmental and climate policies. The mutual recognition of religious actors and IGOs is thus a key element in founding what Charles Taylor calls a "modern moral order"[14] based on three principles: respect for the rights and freedoms of all members of society—in this case the international sphere; their equality; and their consent to the rules imposed on all. It should be emphasised that the World Bank dialogue with religious actors should be understood as a normalised trend that is becoming widespread in the field of development rather than as an initiative taken exclusively by religious actors,[15] who do not have the power to directly influence states and IGOs in

[13] David R. Smock, *Religious Contributions to Peacemaking: When Religion Brings Peace, Not War*, Washington, DC, Institute of Peace, 2006. R. Scott Appleby, *The Ambivalence of the Sacred: Religion, Violence, and Reconciliation*, Lanham, MD, Rowman & Littlefield Publishers, 2000.

[14] Charles Taylor, *Modern Social Imaginaries*, Durham, Duke University Press, 2004. See also the comment by Gerard Clark, "Faith Matters: Faith-Based Organisations, Civil Society and International Development", *Journal of International Development*, 18, 2006, p. 845: "it's worth remembering that 'development' is itself a normative ideal and moral cause, and as such has much in common with the faith discourses from which it has traditionally remained aloof".

[15] The Alliance of Religion and Conservation (ARC) which co-founded a network of faith groups working on ecological and development issues have played an important role in establishing work relationships between the World Bank and faith-based organisations. See the President of the World Bank, James D. Wolfensohn's foreword in Martin

their development policies. Religious action in the international context is therefore part of a norm: a legal and ethical framework that promotes the development of such action.

What is at stake for religious actors is therefore not their recognition on the international scene, but the translation into action of the IGOs' discourses. And most of them wished they had been invited to participate in the various debates and decisions on the climate, as evinced by some of their press releases. Such distancing in cooperative actions carried out with religious actors can be explained by factors endogenous to any organisation such as lack of support from the organisation's executives.[16] However, what needs to be further stressed is that even if IGOs can be specialised agency of the United Nations system such as the World Bank, they do depend on member states' domestic policies. Admittedly, as an autonomous organisation[17]—but linked to the UN through cooperative activities—the World Bank for instance is still subject to international regulation by states, which remain central actors in UN international development policies. States remain at the head of international public policies because the UN system is built that way. It seems therefore appropriate to examine the change in powerful states' internal political choices. Do we need to consider also a (re-)positioning shift on the part of religious leaders themselves? In any event, the answers to these questions should not minimise the significance of the "religious turnaround" in the field of international relations.

Even the realist theory itself engaged with this "religious turnaround" in the 1990s with the publication of Samuel Huntington's first article in *Foreign Affairs*.[18] Huntington wondered about future civilisational conflict—expressed in the form of a question: "The Clash of Civilizations?", which later became a definite affirmation in the title of his book. In his latest work, we see the rise of new theories of (in)security in international relations that developed at the end of the Cold War with the

---

Palmer with Victoria Finlay, *Faith in Conservation. New approaches to Religions and the Environment*, Washington, DC, The World Bank, 2003.

[16] McDuie-Ra and Rees (2010: 26).

[17] Michael Barnett & Martha Finnemore, *Rules for the World*, Cornell, 2004.

[18] Samuel P. Huntington, "The Clash of Civilizations?", *Foreign Affairs*, 72 (3), 1993, pp. 22–49.

fall of the Soviet regime.[19] That bipolar world is long gone, and for the proponents of the clash of civilisations theory, religion—Islam in particular—has become a new enemy for the Western bloc, both externally and from within, especially through the image of the Muslim migrant. The discipline of political science and international relations has consequently become more interested in the influence of religion on the local political scene.[20] Yet, it should be emphasised that the scientific focus on "religion in international relations" has gradually been intensifying in the social sciences.[21] This is notably the case of studies on faith-based NGOs and/or church representatives who became advocacy actors when their exchanges with IGO leaders involved challenging and criticising the direction taken in international public development policies. Arguably, when religions become social movements, there is no longer room for dialogue between religions and official (i.e. inter-state) development actors. Religious actors remain relevant counterparts for intergovernmental organisations when they are in tune with the dominant ideas and practices in the development field dominated by IGO and state policies.[22] It is obvious here that the boundary between secular and religious does not enable us to study the different hybrid forms of counter-hegemonic action or the mobilisation of religions on the local and international scene. The sacred and the secular are mutually, but never separately, constituted in the field of development, and both are also dependent on the role the state can play.

Changes are also taking place in the religious field. It is the growing visibility of faith-based NGOs on the local and international scene that can also foster changes in the field of religion and which also explains researchers' growing interest in this particular issue of religion and development. All religions invite their believers and devotees to help their loved

---

[19] Didier Bigo, "Grands Débats dans un Petit Monde", *Cultures & Conflits* (19–20), 1995 [online].

[20] Shireen T. Hunter, *God on Our Side. Religion in International Affairs*, Londres, Rowman & Littlefield, 2017.

[21] Tanya B. Schwarz & Cecelia Lynch, "Religion in International Relations", *Oxford Research Encyclopedia of Politics*, November 2016. https://doi.org/10.1093/acrefore/9780190228637.013.122.

[22] (McDuie-Ra and Rees 2010: 31). In their analysis, the writers of this article take into account Nandy's words: "the state 'always prefers to deal with religious ideologies rather than with faiths'".

ones and the most destitute. Action in favour of the poor is nothing new for religions and faith-based organisations. It is, however, the rise of civil society on the local scene in the context of democratisation or resistance to the authoritarian state that has helped promote the visibility of its members such as religious actors. The World Bank estimates that in sub-Saharan Africa, nearly 50% of services in the fields of health and education are provided by faith-based NGOs.[23] The failure of a number of neoliberal economic policies has finally enabled these confessional organisations to participate in the "privatisation of the State" and to carry out development initiatives in parallel with state programmes, either in cooperation with the state or independently.

Beyond the approach of a functionalist survey on the theme of religion and development, it is now appropriate to address the complex aspects that have shaped the discussion on the relationship between religion and sustainable development since the early 2000s. The socio-historical and critical analysis is an element to be taken into account in this study. The perspective of international political sociology has therefore been adopted to understand the ways in which religions work for sustainable development and to grasp their doctrinal, political and social approaches to sustainable development on the international scene. This approach is of course shaped by translocal dynamics, which must now be analysed with a particular scientific focus on the advocacy and actions taken by religions to address the issue of climate change.

CLIMATE AND INTERNATIONAL RELATIONS: NEXUS OF CLIMATE CHANGE, ENVIRONMENT AND DEVELOPMENT

The relationship between the climate, environment and development is gradually becoming acknowledged in international awareness and policies. The discourse around the climate will become increasingly tightly linked to the objectives of sustainable development—for scientific reasons, primarily, but also as part of the international agenda. First of all, in terms of scientific facts, global warming threatens not only the quality of the air we breathe as a consequence of urban and industrial pollution, but also the atmospheric system and water cycles, along with biodiversity. Global warming resulting from human action, which has increased the release of

---

[23] Ben Jones and Marie Juul Petersen (2011: 1293).

greenhouse gases (GHGs) into the atmosphere[24] since the age of industrialisation in the nineteenth century therefore generally threatens not only the environment but also the development capacities of nations. Climate change is therefore a global and complex problem which, although environmental in nature, has impacts of global dimensions on features such as health, poverty, the economy, population growth, resource management and peace; and it obviously has geopolitical consequences such as migratory flows.

The adaptation of individuals, groups and (agricultural) territories to climate change remains part of the global objectives of sustainable development, but it is also a major societal and political challenge. This is notably the stance taken by the All Africa Conference of Churches (AACC), a faith-based and ecumenical African continental organisation. The AACC has observer status within the African Union and was noteworthy in particular for its action in favour of peace building and interreligious dialogue in East Africa in the early 2000s. In a document entitled "Report of the Study on African Ecumenical Engagement with the Consultation Process Towards a Joint EU-Africa Strategy", dating back to 2007, the AACC states, for example, that food security is a major issue in the framework of the partnership between the European Union and Africa. It nevertheless affirms the significance of the colonial legacy on the continent development policies.[25] The principle of common but differentiated responsibility, recognised by the UNFCCC and in the Kyoto Protocol (I will elaborate on this later) is upheld by the AACC, but also by developing countries in general, even in their economic governance. Over the past five years, a new discourse has been developing in the UN system, focusing mainly on shared responsibility. An example would be the issue of migration that has resulted from climate change,

---

[24] GHGs are the gaseous constituents that trap heat in the atmosphere. GHGs are released through natural processes (e.g. decomposition of biomass) and as a result of human activity (e.g. the burning of fossil fuels). Carbon dioxide (CO_2) is the largest single contributor to climate change.

See the document entitled "Why Nature ? Why Now ? How nature is key to achieving a 1.5 °C world", The Food and Land Use Coalition, October 2021. https://www.foo dandlandusecoalition.org/why-nature/.

[25] "Report of the Study on African Ecumenical Engagement with the Consultation Process Towards a Joint EU-Africa Strategy", All Africa Conference of Churches, Nairobi, October 2007 https://europafrica.files.wordpress.com/2007/11/report-of-the-study-on-joint-eu-africa-strategy.pdf, consulted on 24 January 2020.

which continues to create challenges for agriculture. The phenomenon of migration must henceforth also be approached in terms of its environmental dimension and not only in economic terms, as migrant refugees are likely to represent a new migratory and political phenomenon for a large number of the states within the international system, such as those in Africa.[26] This is one reason among many others why the Global Compact for Safe, Orderly and Regular Migration was adopted by the international community in December 2018 in Marrakech. This is in line with the international sustainable development agenda which emphasises the responsibility of all for the good of all in a cooperative governance framework.

Addressing climate change nowadays involves international or global public policies embodied in the UN's sustainable development goals adopted in 2015. Therefore, sustainable development cannot be considered as the strict equivalent of the development analysed so far. Indeed, sustainable development, just like climate action, implies learning how to "steer the human enterprise",[27] not only in the South but everywhere on the Earth. And this steering process is complex because of the consequences of climate change in environmental terms. These consequences also seriously impact on the atmosphere, oceans, mountains and species biodiversity, which religions enshrine in their sacred scriptures under the principle of respect for life. Religious actors such as the national Muslim organisation, the Muslim Judicial Council (MJC) in South Africa, stressed the urgency of protecting biodiversity and deplored the failure to act in

---

[26] It is, for example, estimated that there will be 200 million climate change refugees by 2050, according to the research findings of Prof. Norman Myers. Quoted by Ross Michael Pink, *The Climate Change Crisis. Solutions and Adaption for a Planet in Peril*, Palgrave Macmillan, 2018, p. 2. Susan, Martin, "Climate Change, Migration, and Governance", *Global Governance*, 16 (3), 2010, pp. 397–414.

[27] Robert Kandel, "Le débat se réchauffe", in Jacques Theys & Bernard Kalaora (eds.), *La Terre outragée. Les experts sont formels !*, Paris, Editions Autrement, 1992, pp. 104–110.

Muslim circles as well as in international forums.[28] This issue of biodiversity was finally addressed in the 2021 Glasgow Climate Pact of COP 26.[29] This might perhaps coincide with IUCN (International Union for Conservation of Nature) World Conservation Congress held in Marseille during the same year, in September 2021. Climate change and biodiversity, as asserted by Laurence Tubiana, an architect of the Paris Agreement, are linked and now acknowledged as such by international institutions.[30] It is worth mentioning that the oceans, considered as sinks for absorbing CO_2,[31] were also mentioned in the Glasgow Climate Pact as an ecosystem whose protection must be ensured in the same way as forests or the cryosphere are protected. Religious actors have therefore proved to be in line with major international decisions taken some years after their mobilisation for biodiversity.

Global warming is not only causing a rise in the levels of the ocean, which covers about 70% of the planet's surface, but it also threatens, among other things, to melt the earth's ice caps. The international community represented by the United Nations has often insisted that there is a risk to islands and coastal areas in Bangladesh and China, among other places. For the common good, it is imperative that a solution to the melting of the ice caps be found. The melting of Antarctica has been on

---

[28] The main spokesperson of the MJC on this issue is Sheikh Muhammad Ridwaan Gallant, Imam with whom I conducted interviews in 2015 and 2020. In particular, he had organised events on the sidelines of COP 17 in Durban to raise awareness among citizens and South African institutional actors. He has since created a website promoting pro-environmental actions with reference to Islamic thought and in favour of regulation. See in particular his position on respect for biodiversity and the denunciation of rhinoceros poaching in Africa: https://mridwaangallant.wordpress.com/.

[29] "*Recognizing* the interlinked global crises of climate change and biodiversity loss, and the critical role of protecting, conserving and restoring nature and ecosystems in delivering benefits for climate adaptation and mitigation, while ensuring social and environmental safeguards". Decision -/CP.26 Glasgow Climate Pact.

[30] Laurence Tubiana: "More and more we will see that it is impossible to distinguish between biodiversity and climate. They're two parts of the same problem" (https://www.climatechangenews.com/2021/11/11/nature-based-solutions-prove-divisive-glasgow-climate-talks/).

[31] See the document entitled "Why Nature? Why Now? How nature is key to achieving a 1.5 °C world", The Food and Land Use Coalition, October 2021. https://www.foodandlandusecoalition.org/why-nature/.

the international political agenda since 2005.[32] Prior to that, the 1959 Antarctic Treaty prohibited the conduct of military activities, the presence of nuclear weapons and the disposing of nuclear waste there to prevent the accelerated melting of the ice. The Antarctic does not belong to any state and commercial and strategic stakes are supposed to be barely relevant (except in terms of scientific research). However, things seem to be different for the Arctic.[33] In recent years, it has become an issue for world powers and control over it can give Russia the opportunity to develop a new sea route, the Northern Route, for the transit of commercial goods, which is less expensive than shipping goods via the Suez Canal. This issue of state power, the flagship concept of the realist theory and the defence of national interests remain obstacles to multilateral climate negotiations and have been denounced by religious actors in numerous statements.

The international agenda has certainly been deeply impacted by the balance of power among states, but also between state and non-state actors. However, the interdependence[34] and interactions that characterise the context of globalisation also refer to the cooperation in international relations that is so vital to reducing anthropogenic-related greenhouse gas (GHG) emissions. It was only in 2010 that governments agreed that GHG emissions must be decreased so that the increase in global temperature should be kept to 2 degrees Celsius. Later, in 2018, the IPCC produced a special report on the impacts of global warming of 1.5 °C above pre-industrial levels.

The consequences at the level of islands states are considered extremely serious for the inhabitants and indigenous populations already organising themselves, setting up associations to make their voices heard and defend the sacredness of their territories. The alarm was raised by the Indian Ocean islands particularly at the 2012 Conference of the Parties (COP) in Doha. States that own these Indian Ocean islands such as the Maldives signalled the urgency of the need for countermeasures to be taken. However, a power game is being played, which is denounced by

---

[32] Olave Schram Stokke & Davor Vidas, *Governing the Antarctic: The Effectiveness and Legitimacy of the Antarctic Treaty System*, Cambridge, 1997.

[33] Anthony, Giddens, *The Politics of Climate Change*, Cambridge, Polity Press, 2011, pp. 203–204.

[34] Bruce Russett & John Oneal, *Triangulating Peace: Democracy, Interdependence, and International Organizations*, New York, Norton, 2000.

civil society actors and activists commenting on the perceived ineffectiveness of the various COPs. Religious actors can also belong to secular NGOs dedicated to defending the territorial claims of indigenous peoples. Advocacy networks represented by NGOs, such as the Indigenous Peoples of Africa as well as the South African San Institute, play a role within the framework of the COPs.[35] The weakest states in terms of power capability and occupying a territory at risk of being submerged are well aware of the limits of the international community's promises of solidarity in the face of their vulnerabilities.[36] However, they can still voice their concerns and claims for climate justice by hosting UNFCCC's COPs. It is essential to understand this issue of the impact of power capabilities on states on the international scene when it comes, for example, to volunteering to organise the COPs. The Fiji Islands chaired COP 23 not on their national territory but in Bonn, where the United Nations Framework Convention on Climate Change (UNFCCC) offices are located, because of the impossibility (for security reasons) for the country to host such an international event.

The environment is a global public good,[37] which implies the need for cooperation and reciprocity. However, things are not so simple because, with the globalisation of the economy, power games (balance of power, hegemonic power, etc.) are being reactivated. States therefore seek to minimise environmental risks in order to pursue their own development and strengthen their own economic power, as illustrated by the case of the United States with the Trump administration's decision to withdraw from the Paris Agreement and the controversies that ensued. However, minimising environmental risks dates back to the origins of climate negotiations. These negotiations have been organised within the framework of the United Nations system since the 1990s. Countries from the South and

---

[35] Nigel Crawhall, a Buddhist interviewed in 2015, 2019 and 2020, has notably dedicated himself to defending indigenous peoples' territorial claims by advocating within these organisations and within the framework of the COPs.

[36] These states have set up funds for the purchase of land in another country to house their inhabitants, as shown by the example of the Kiribati archipelago, which has a refuge territory in the Fiji archipelago.

[37] About global public good, see among others (Marie-Claude, Smouts, "Du patrimoine commun de l'humanité aux biens publics globaux", in Cormier-Salem, Marie-Christine et al. (eds.), *Patrimoines naturels au Sud: Territoires, identités et strategies locales* [online], Marseille, IRD Editions, 2005, pp. 53–70), Le développement durable. Les termes du débat, Paris, Armand Colin, collection, *Compact civis*

the North have sought to protect their strategic interests and economic development. The Kyoto Protocol, however, did not provide common aims and strategies for all states responsible for greenhouse gas emissions.

Conferences of the Parties (COPs) of the UNFCCC: The Climate Negotiations

During some of the climate negotiations organised by the UNFCCC within the COP framework states tend to act as "stowaways", in the sense that the stowaway's behaviour, for a country, entails waiting for others to make the effort to limit their GHG emissions rather than trying to do so itself. However, according to the SternReview,[38] climate change mitigation requires new economic tools to soften the impact of climate change and enable an immediate reduction in GHG emissions for the sake of generating economic benefits at the international level that are far greater than the cost of mitigation policies.[39]

In spite of these recommendations, some questions can be asked about the global economic context and more particularly about the role of companies and multinational firms. What do companies decide in the face of the politicisation of the environmental issue? They can, for example, threaten to withdraw from countries identified as being too demanding in environmental matters through a strategy of delocalisation. The lobby of large industries exploiting non-renewable fossil fuels was harshly criticised by civil society and religious actors, such as South African Anglican Archbishop Desmond Tutu. He has supported the transnational mobilisation of civil society for disinvestment in companies of fossil fuels. Tutu's commitment through online networks expressed a firm stand in favour of these disinvestment campaigns. He thereby provided moral support to these transnational movements, comparing them to the boycotts and disinvestment of Western companies that invested in South

---

[38] Nicholas Stern, *The Economics of Climate Change: The Stern Review*, Cambridge, Cambridge University Press, 2007.

[39] According to Ross M. Pink, the World Bank considered in 2010 that each year USD 70 to 100 billion will be required for effective mitigation action compared to USD 700 billion to 1 trillion representing the annual destructive cost of climate change (Pink 2018: 3).

Africa during apartheid.[40] Since then and ahead of COP 26, which took place in November 2021 in Glasgow, 72 faith institutions have made the largest-ever divestment announcement.[41] Religious actors today claim that financial investments in fossil fuels represent one of the strongest driving forces in the current capitalist system. Therefore, divesting from companies that extract and burn fossil fuels is seen by religious institutions which are also stakeholders and investors as one of the key avenues to address the climate crisis.[42]

Clearly, the reciprocity and interdependence that liberal theorists have insisted on is difficult to realise because of the economic and specifically capitalist interests and power in international relations. This has shown the extent to which the economic sphere is impacted by the context of financial interests, where the main climate actors have developed new strategies such as the faith disinvestment network. The first climate actor and the one which can express and amplify religious actors' discourse on climate change is the United Nations system, responsible for managing global public goods. It is the UN and its subsidiary bodies that clearly carry out actions in the field of the environment and climate change within the framework of international conferences and which can partner with faith-based organisations. In accordance with the liberal theoretical perspective, the protection of common interests cannot be achieved over the short term but only over the long term. States are therefore justified in projecting their climate agendas in a long-term perspective when setting up their environmental and development public policies. However, as we

---

[40] "Desmond Tutu: we fought apartheid. Now climate change is our global enemy" (https://www.theguardian.com/commentisfree/2014/sep/21/desmond-tutu-climate-change-is-the-global-enemy). Some excerpts from his 2014 statement shed light on the issue of the boycott of fossil fuels, for example: "The destruction of the earth's environment is the human rights challenge of our time. ... The most devastating effects are visited on the poor, those with no involvement in creating the problem. A deep injustice. Just as we argued in the 1980s that those who conducted business with apartheid South Africa were aiding and abetting an immoral system, today we say nobody should profit from the rising temperatures, seas and human suffering caused by the burning of fossil fuels". See S. Sadouni, "L'action interreligieuse pour le climat", *Histoire, monde & cultures religieuses*, 2016, n° 40.

[41] https://operationnoah.org/featured/gda2021/.

[42] See Research Report funded by the Keeling Curve Prize "Cooler Earth. Higher Benefits. Actions by Those Who Care About Children, Climate and Finance", Geneva, WCC (World Council of Churches), 2021 (second edition), p. 12.

shall see, the international situation is much more complex because multilateral negotiations on climate change, and especially within the Kyoto Protocol framework, ultimately have to confront a divide between developed and developing countries. Moreover, developed countries fear that the ecological transition will not yield its expected rewards in terms of job creation nor curb the rise of extremist populism.

First, it is necessary to examine how the disconnect between developed and developing countries could have materialised? We need to start by looking at the Kyoto Protocol, which was adopted on 11 December 1997 and entered into force on 16 February 2005. This description and analysis will also enable us to synthesise the different stages of the international agenda for the issues of climate change and sustainable development in order to establish the global context of religious actors' pro-climate discourse and actions. This is in line with the objectives of a constructivist sociology. Religious actors interviewed have firmly underlined in their remarks the need to remedy what was missing in the Kyoto Protocol in the new Paris Agreement.

The Kyoto Protocol

The first milestones in responding to the global warming challenge date back to 1990, the year of the first IPCC report. According to the analysis cited above in this chapter, the climate, the environment and sustainable development are tightly linked and interconnected. We need to go back three decades earlier to understand the main steps that led to the creation of the United Nations Framework Convention on Climate Change (UNFCCC). This retrospective view has often been highlighted by religious actors themselves and, for example, by those in charge of climate issues within transnational organisations such as the World Council of Churches (WCC) based in Geneva but also by IFEES (Islamic Foundation for Ecology and Environmental Sciences).[43] It helps to understand the changes in the domain of international climate action[44]:

[43] We can mention the book of the founder of IFEES, Fazlun M. Khalid, *Signs on the Earth. Islam, Modernity and the Climate Crisis*, Kube Publishing, 2019.

[44] Interviews with Guillermo Kerber in Lyon in November 2015. During the conference co-organised in Lyon on "Religious Actors and Climate Change", he emphasised, the importance of the 1992 Earth Summit as a fundamental step in conveying the voice of Christian religious actors on the international scene. Guillermo Kerber now teaches

the macrocosm that enables us to better analyse religious cosmopolitanism within the transnational field of climate engagements (see Chapters 2, 4 and 5). The first multilateral meetings were the Earth Summits organised since 1972, when the first one, the United Nations Conference on the Human Environment held in Stockholm, led to the creation of UNEP (United Nations Environment Programme) based in Nairobi.[45] The Earth Summit is a conference organised every ten years by the United Nations to exchange views on global policies for sustainable development. The Earth Summit called Rio+20 (United Nations Conference on Sustainable Development Rio+20) took place in Rio de Janeiro in 2012. During this international event, a final declaration was adopted by heads of states and governments as well as high-level representatives in favour of the Sustainable Development 2030 Agenda. This culminated three years later in September 2015, at the United Nations General Assembly, in the final document "Transforming our world: the Sustainable Development Agenda 2030", better known as Agenda 2030, which sets out 17 sustainable development goals. A few months later, in December 2015, the international community endorsed the Paris Agreement which commits states to, among other things, moving towards an economy based on net-zero carbon emissions by the second half of the century.

The UNFCCC was created during the 1992 UN Conference on Environment and Development, also held in Rio de Janeiro, to consider what could be done to reduce global warming and deal with any unavoidable rise in temperature. Signatory countries have been meeting annually since 1995. We need to start by looking at this brief chronological account: what does it teach us? First of all, the COP 21 that led to the Paris Agreement was only one step in a process that began more than forty years before, with the first 1972 Stockholm Earth Summit. Secondly, multilateralism is a mechanism whose effects are felt over the long term only, although scientists have repeatedly stressed the urgency

---

at the Ecumenical Theology Workshop in Switzerland and is also the author of articles and books on ecology and theology. See in particular, G. Kerber, "International Advocacy for Climate Justice", in R. Globus Veldman, A. Szasz & R. Haluza-DeLay, *How the World's Religions are Responding to Climate Change: Social Scientific Investigations*, London, Routledge, 2016; G. Kerber, "A Response to Wesley Granberg-Michaelson", in Ernst Conradie & Hilda Koster (eds.), *T&T Clark Handbook of Christian Theology and Climate Change*, London Bloomsbury, 2020, pp. 351–356.

[45] See, among others, Lorraine Elliot, *The Global Politics of the Environment*, New York, Palgrave Macmillan, 2004.

of the situation. These experts are not only from the IPCC, because the first international experts to work on climate were meteorologists in the International Meteorological Organization, established in 1879 as a non-governmental organisation in charge of international exchanges of meteorological data.[46] In 1951, it became the World Meteorological Organization (WMO), a specialised agency within the United Nations system. Later, in 1988, the IPCC was created by the WMO and UNEP. It is therefore the United Nations, for all its many flaws, that is implementing various climate initiatives and has laid the foundations for the adoption of the Kyoto Protocol under the UNFCCC. The Protocol was overtaken by the whirlwind of international affairs and in particular by the contested power relations inherent in the successive international systems.

A series of negotiations therefore began within the Conferences of Parties (COP) of the UNFCCC to find a solution to climate change. In 1997, the Kyoto Protocol was adopted during COP 3 held in Kyoto, Japan. However, the protocol came into force only in 2005 because, among other things, it had to be ratified by at least 55 countries to be applicable. At that time, there were 182 States or Parties at the UNFCCC, while today there are 197—with the COPs as decision-making bodies. The European Union had ratified the Kyoto Protocol, unlike the United States, despite being the largest greenhouse gas emitter at that time. The COPs that follow one another annually had the objective of setting the modalities for the implementation of the protocol, and it is actually the same process for the Paris Agreement since 2015.

At that time, the Kyoto Protocol contained measures that were legally binding on Northern developed countries.[47] However, the first constraint period began in 2008 and was to end in 2012. At the 17th Conference of the Parties (COP 17) to the UNFCCC, which took place in Durban in 2011, the governments of the Parties to the Kyoto Protocol decided that a second constraint period would be established, starting in 2012 and lasting until 2020, which was the last year for a new

---

[46] See the WMO site in French https://public.wmo.int/fr/%C3%A0-propos-de-nous/qui-sommes-nous/histoire-de-lomm.

[47] Jana, Von Stein, "The International Law and Politics of Climate Change: Ratification of the United Nations Framework Convention and the Kyoto Protocol", *Journal of Conflict Resolution*, 52 (2), 2008, pp. 243–268; Michael Grubb & Duncan Brack (publishers.), *The Kyoto Protocol: A Guide and Assessment*, Royal Institute of International Affairs, 1999.

agreement. The following year, in Doha and during COP 18, the Doha Amendment to the Kyoto Protocol confirmed this second commitment period.[48] The Paris Agreement was finally adopted in 2015.[49]

During the various COPs organised until 2011, a polarisation between different countries intensified: the United States and emerging countries such as China emphasised the defence of their national interests, which they considered as threatened by incentives for climate mitigation. Europe, on the other hand, was more accommodating by playing a role in supporting multilateral negotiations[50] and the Kyoto Protocol. Concretely, the Protocol was the first legally binding international agreement in which participating nations (mainly industrialised countries) committed to implementing emission control targets, namely an average 5% reduction in GHG emissions from 2008 to 2012 compared to 1990 levels.

Yet, from the outset the scope of the Kyoto Protocol was limited by the US Congress's refusal to ratify it. To this limitation must be added the fact that Japan, Canada and Russia also failed to ratify it (Russia did so in 2004), and the Protocol could not act on their GHG emissions, which were the highest in the world. It was only after Russia's ratification in 2004 that the treaty was able to take effect in 2005 because the States (Parties) to the Kyoto Protocol were supposed to account for 55% of the world's GHG emissions. The Paris Agreement on Climate Change, negotiated at COP 21, commits 187 of the 197 Parties to the Convention to ratify it.[51] It has since become a legally binding international treaty on climate change. The agreement was intended to limit global warming to below 2 °C, preferably 1.5 °C, compared to pre-industrial levels.[52] To reflect the "principle of common but differentiated responsibility" that governs climate negotiations, the Kyoto Protocol was therefore designed

[48] https://unfccc.int/kyoto_protocol (consulted 17 December 2021).

[49] https://unfccc.int/sites/default/files/resource/docs/2011/cop17/eng/09a01.pdf.

[50] M. Paterson, "Post-hegemonic Climate Politics?", *British Journal of Politics and International Relations*, 11, 2009, pp. 140–158.

[51] https://unfccc.int/process/the-paris-agreement/status-of-ratification (consulted on 7 November 2019).

[52] The French Parliament passed Law No. 2016-786 of June 15, 2016, authorising the ratification of the Paris Agreement adopted on December 12, 2015, which requires the entire European Union to do the same.

according to a binary logic. One the one hand, because of their historical responsibility for climate change, industrialised countries had to meet
GHG emission reduction targets. On the other hand, countries benefiting
in 1990 from their "developing country" status escaped these constraints.
In concrete terms, this meant that emerging economies such as China,
India, Brazil and South Africa were exempt from any binding quantitative
targets. China, in particular, had been able to negotiate its own economic
interests in the best possible way during these various multilateral meetings.[53] As the largest GHG emitter since 2007, it was nevertheless facing
growing pressure from Western industrialised countries, which argued the
special status it enjoyed under the Kyoto Protocol was no longer justified
due to its growing economic weight.[54]

During the negotiations that followed the ratification of the Kyoto
Protocol, first the United States, then the European Union constantly
called for the extension of GHG reduction targets to emerging countries.
This binary logic of the Kyoto Protocol was therefore seriously criticised
by industrialised countries, particularly because the exclusion of large
countries from the global emissions trading system made no economic
sense.[55] On the other hand, emerging countries have constantly claimed
their right to development. It should also be recalled that religious institutions in Africa, such as the ecumenical AACC, had supported the principle
of "differentiated responsibility" in development and environmental policies, a principle that had intensified the difficulties encountered by UN
officials in their dealings with both Northern and Southern state actors.
According to the religious actors present at the conference co-organised
in Lyon on "Religious actors and climate change" in 2015, UNFCCC
members were experiencing almost daily stress in their professional lives.
On the one hand, scientific experts were alerting them to the "tragic"
consequences of climate change, yet on the other hand, they had to
mobilise the Parties to the UNFCCC to carry out policies to mitigate
GHG emissions.

[53] Interview with G. M., former South African negotiator at various COPs, 14 February
2020.

[54] See Blandine Barreau & Johanne Buba, "La Chine dans le processus de Copenh-
ague: la difficile inclusion d'un grand emergent", in Jean Tirole, *Politique climatique: une
nouvelle architecture internationale*, Ministère du développement durable, Paris, 2009.

[55] (Barreau & Buba 2009).

North/South Divide

After the adoption of the Kyoto Protocol, countries in the North felt that developing countries should not be allowed to play the role of stowaways at the expense of richer countries, some of which have been trying to curb their GHG emissions.[56] The North considered that the new technologies (called green technologies) that will allow industries and companies to be less polluting will be able to amortise the costs related to the reduction of GHGs in the long term. Moreover, as developed countries in the North, they believed developing countries were likely to benefit economically from the Kyoto Protocol[57] if it were renewed and made generally applicable on the world stage. Developing countries would thus be in a position to sell their "emission permits" to other countries, a provision allowing them to sell or buy emission rights among industrialized countries. Only developed countries were targeted by the Protocol's emission quotas, while developing countries were exempt. However, the carbon market—so called because carbon dioxide (CO_2) is the most widely produced greenhouse gas and also because the emissions of other GHGs are recorded and accounted for in terms of carbon equivalents—could be flexible in terms of the price per ton of CO_2. The price therefore had to be prohibitive for developing countries to benefit from the carbon market. Nevertheless, for some experts in economic development in the South, the carbon market represented an advantageous mechanism, as in the case of South Africa.[58] In fact, and according to carbon market

[56] See more particularly Joshua S. Goldstein & Jon C. Pevehouse, *International Relations*, Pearson, 2013, and more particularly the section "Let's Debate the Issue": "Stopping Global Warming: Who Should Pay?", pp. 422–423.

[57] According to Clive L. Spash, "the targets under the Kyoto Protocol have been framed as part of an economic discourse where priority is given to creating gains from trade, extending the roles of markets, and protecting the profits of potentially vulnerable polluters. (…) What should be clear is that regulatory instruments (whether taxes, permits, or direct regulation are not neutral either politically or ideologically. They play to specific groups within society". Clive L. Spash, "Carbon Trading: A Critique", in J.S. Dryzek, R.B. Norgaard, & D. Schlosberg, *The Oxford Handbook of Climate Change and Society*, Oxford, Oxford University Press, 2011, p. 558.

[58] Interview with Ivor Sarakinsky, a former official of the South African Ministry of Economy and Development (Economic Development Department) and in charge of green economy issues in Johannesburg, 24 Feb 2020. See also, Ivor Sarakinsky, "Recognition and Obligation: EU and South Africa Renewable Energy Development Cooperation", GLOBUS, Research Paper 5/2019, October 2019.

laws, the higher the cost, the greater the economic pressure on major GHG-emitting countries. The latter would therefore be encouraged to use energy more efficiently or to invest in renewable energies that emit few or no GHGs. It is difficult to know whether a carbon market with a high price per ton of CO_2 could be an advantageous device for developing countries and for the mitigation of GHG emissions.[59]

In the framework of the Paris Agreement, it is the adoption of financial mechanisms that have been favoured in order to help developing countries make their ecological transition.[60] The financial mechanism is the result of a common agreement between the Parties to the UNFCCC. However, the challenge, even today, is how to implement this mechanism. So, a new agreement has to strike a balance between all these requirements and finally acknowledge China's status as a major economic power. Moreover, the path towards the adoption of the Paris Agreement could not have been achieved without prior dialogue between the United States and China, which has become the second world economic power since the early 2000s.[61]

The Paris Agreement remains historic, because it made possible a compromise acceptable to developing countries, grouped notably within the G77, and developed countries. Moreover, it maintained a binding mechanism based on the obligation of states to establish a national contribution, i.e. a precise commitment to reduce GHG emissions. Religious leaders, like those of the Orthodox Church, have often criticised the Kyoto Protocol limits and the refusal to ratify it by all the major GHG-emitting countries. On the eve of COP 22, the Ecumenical Patriarch, in his message sent to the UNFCCC, called for political leadership to be held accountable for "our ecological sins"[62] after 22 years of inertia.

---

[59] (Spash 2011).

[60] Article 9.1 of the Paris Agreement stipulates: "Developed country Parties shall provide financial resources to assist developing country Parties with respect to both mitigation and adaptation in continuation of their existing obligations under the Convention".

[61] A. Giddens, *The Politics of Climate Change*, op. cit., pp. 222–224.

[62] I would like to thank Archbishop Serafim of Zimbabwe who enabled me to consult the message of Patriarch Bartholomew I in view of the COP 22 organised in Marrakech. I quote excerpts from this message: "For twenty-two years, then, the world's leading authorities and politicians have fundamentally agreed on the problems of global climate change and have held endless consultations and high-level conversations on something that requires practical measures and tangible action. Twenty-two years, however, is an

The call for repentance for "ecological sins" is becoming more and more common in the discourse of Christian actors and in particular in the various WCC communiqués.[63] As far as Muslims are concerned, what was emphasised years before COP 21 was rather the responsibility of the believer (*mu'min*), the guarantor of a collective safeguard.[64] Recently, an Islamic text—*Al Mizan A Covenant for the Earth*—is in the process of being adopted by Muslim organisations through global consultation and will be submitted to the Organisation of Islamic Cooperation[65] (see Chapter 4).

The Paris Agreement

Since the adoption of the Paris Agreement in December 2015 within the framework of the UN Climate Conference,[66] new commitments have been made by states to limit global warming to well below 2 degrees Celsius, preferably to 1.5 °C, compared to pre-industrial levels.

The Kyoto Protocol failed, as we have seen, because it included only 55% of the GHG emissions of the countries that ratified it. As soon as the Protocol was adopted in 1997, the United States refused to take part

---

unacceptably long period to respond to the environmental crisis, especially when we are conscious of its intimate and inseparable connections to global poverty, migration and unrest. (...) After twenty-two years, it is finally time – and long overdue – for all of us to discern the human faces impacted by ecological sins". "Message by His All-Holiness Ecumenical Patriarch Bartholomew To the UNFCCC COP 22 Session – Marrakech, Morocco, November 7–18, 2016".

[63] https://www.oikoumene.org/en/what-we-do/climate-change/activity_news?b_start:int=250 (consulted on 28 January 2020).

[64] These are also the words of Husna Ahmad, head of the London-based NGO Global One, who participated in the conference co-organised in Lyon. Global One aims to raise awareness among Muslim women about climate action in their families and communities. See also her keynote speech at a conference held at Hamad Bin Khalifa University in Doha, Qatar, the Research Center for Islamic Legislation and Ethics (CILE) entitled "CILE 2019 A Global Ethical Approach to Social Justice and Environmental Issues: Ethical Review of Global Environment Status". https://www.cilecenter.org/resources/articles-essays/cile2019-global-ethical-approach-social-justice-and-environmental-issues (consulted on 28 January 2020).

[65] Interview with Fazlun M. Khalid, 22 June 2021.

[66] Pascal Canfin, Peter Staime, *Climat, 30 questions pour comprendre la conférence de Paris*, Paris, Les petits matins, 2015.

in it even though the country was responsible for 20% of GHG emissions on its own. The Kyoto Protocol was therefore quickly outdated, as we have seen, also because of the differentiation between developed and developing countries that was no longer reflecting the changes in the international system. The Protocol was renewed in 2012 for a further 8 years. It was one year before that the international community had to start thinking about a new agreement at the COP 17 in Durban, one that would integrate all the parties to the UNFCCC and that finally replace the Kyoto Protocol. China and the United States, the two new economic powers, had shown already signs at this time of cooperation and support for the new agreement to be discussed in Paris. This has been further developed and realised with the recent bilateral agreement at the end of COP 26 at Glasgow in November 2021.

It is the special working group of the Durban Platform for Enhanced Action (DPA), created in the framework of COP 17, that prepared, among other things, the terms of the new agreement under the UNFCCC. The DPA had two main objectives: the first was to develop another legal instrument applicable to all Parties to the Convention, and the second was to increase the level of ambition to mitigate climate change of all States (Parties) for the so-called pre-2020 period. These ambitions directed at mitigation were of course linked to the scientific expertise that produced the IPCC reports.[67]

Mitigation and adaptation goals were debated during the Durban talks and encouraged by the island and developing countries gathered within the Alliance of Small Island States (AOSIS). They wished to maintain the temperature increase at 1.5 °C or 2 °C above pre-industrial levels, without waiting beyond the pre-2020 period. While a new agreement was needed, the AOSIS countries considered that urgent action was necessary to raise the mitigation level and enhance adaptation before 2020. Moreover, it should be stressed that all these discussions on the theme of adaptation were made possible since the adoption, during COP 11, of the Nairobi work programme on impacts, vulnerability and adaptation to climate change. The multilateral debates and negotiations were also aimed

---

[67] Report of the Institut de la Francophonie pour le développement durable (IFDD), "From Paris to Marrakech or the challenge of implementation. Twenty-second Conference of the Parties to the United Nations Framework Convention on Climate Change", Quebec City, Quebec, IFDD, 2016.

at financial, technological and capacity-building support mechanisms for mitigation measures that were finally included in the Paris Agreement.[68]

Unlike the Kyoto Protocol, which contains legally quantified commitments, i.e. binding for the Parties concerned, the Paris Agreement commits all states that have ratified it to take domestic measures to achieve their self-determined objectives. To this end, a technical review process on mitigation, supported by the UNFCCC, was launched, taking into account the most recent scientific data. Decision 1/CP21, paragraph 124 of the Paris Agreement also provided for an evaluation of the technical review process on adaptation measures to be carried out over the 2016–2020 period, with a view to improving its effectiveness. That technical review process was intended to "identify, to the extent possible, concrete opportunities to enhance resilience, reduce vulnerabilities, and increase knowledge and implementation of adaptation measures".[69] Welcomed by many developing countries, adaptation had already at this time become intrinsically linked to mitigation.[70] However, the challenge remains that technologies and practices for mitigation and adaptation need to be widely disseminated. The issue of the Green Fund is therefore becoming central to the sustainability of states' commitments, especially for those in vulnerable situations and needing international assistance for their sustainable development. Non-state actors on the international scene are those who will insist on the notion of climate justice, particularly in the framework of the UNFCCC COPs. The latter can be considered as "hybrid forums"[71] when the debates are not about the Anthropocene, but mainly about the implementation of agreements related to mitigation, adaptation, adopting new green technologies and financing. Religious actors will participate in all of these international forums in order to influence

---

[68] Ibid. It can be seen that these talks were not about trading on the carbon market.

[69] Report by the Institut de la Francophonie pour le développement durable (IFDD), "De Paris à Marrakech ou le défi de la mise en œuvre. Vingt-deuxième Conférence des Parties à la Convention-cadre des Nations Unies sur les changements climatiques", Quebec, IFDD, 2016, p. 17. See also on the IFDD'site: http://www.ifdd.francophonie.org/ressources/ressources-pub.php?id=13.

[70] Interviews with Nigel Crawhall and G. Midgley.

[71] See more particularly Michel Callon & Arie Rip, "Humains, non-humains: morale d'une coexistence", In J. Theys & B. Kalaora (eds.), *La Terre outrage: les experts sont formels!*, Paris, Autrement, 1992, pp. 140–156; Michel Callon, Pierre Lascoumes, Yannick Barthe, *Agir dans un monde incertain. Essai sur la démocratie technique*, Paris, Seuil, 2001.

the debates and deliberations, and then relay to their communities or eco-congresses the international decisions and their critical approaches in favour of climate justice. Together with climate scientists and economists, they will become important actors in the new international climate agenda and within the transnational climate field.

CHAPTER 4

Religious Actions to Address Climate Change: The International Platform

Religious actors have represented a cosmopolitan force by exerting an influence on multilateral negotiations for climate action and sustainable development[1] through their commitments, common declarations, publications and mobilisation, especially during the year 2015, which remains historical. Discourse and action towards ending poverty, protecting the most vulnerable, the environment and the planet are fundamentally ethical and moral by nature.[2] The nature of the mobilisation of religious

---

[1] Michel Sidibé (publishers), Special issue, "Religion and Sustainable Development", *The Review of Faith and International Affairs*, 14 (3), 2016; Clarence Tsimpo & Quentin Wodon, "Faith Affiliation, Religiosity, and Attitudes Towards the Environment and Climate Change", *The Review of Faith & International Affairs*, 14 (3), 2016, pp. 51–64 (https://doi.org/10.1080/15570274.2016.1215850); James R. Cochrane, "Religion in Sustainable Development", *The Review of Faith & International Affairs*, 14 (3), 2016, pp. 89–94 (https://doi.org/10.1080/15570274.2016.1215818); Jenny Lunn, "The Role of Religion, Spirituality and Faith in Development: A Critical Theory Approach", *Third World Quarterly*, 30 (5), 2009, pp. 937–951 (https://doi.org/10.1080/014365 90902959180); Carole Rakodi, "A Framework for Analysing the Links Between Religion and Development", *Development in Practice*, 22(5–6), 2012, pp. 634–650 (https://doi.org/10.1080/09614524.2012.685873).

[2] Anthony Annett, Jeffrey Sachs, Marcelo Sanchez Sorondo, & William Vendley (2017). A Multi-Religious Consensus on the Ethics of Sustainable Development: Reflections of the Ethics in Action Initiative. Economics Discussion Papers, No 2017-56,

---

actors for climate change on the international scene should not be considered as a discrete or marginal case, but as a move that falls within the scope of social action; this invites us to study its modalities, the discourses that support it, and its consequences in different local, national, international and confessional spaces, which are inescapably intertwined[3] (see Chapters 2 and 5). The strength of what is religious and inter-religious lies above all in the capacity for the transnationalisation of a discourse and practices aimed at securing the future of humankind and of the environment.

As we have seen (Chapter 3), the climate encompasses a transborder field of sustainable development where the positions adopted by actors, in particular states, are based—according to realist conceptions of international relations—on issues of power. Why? Because climate action is multi- and transdisciplinary, affecting not only different social, environmental and strategic economic sectors, but also the financial interests that public policymakers sometimes find it difficult to think about jointly, not to mention in moral terms. Even though religious actors such as official mainline churches (Catholic, Orthodox, Protestant, Jewish, Buddhist, Muslim, among others) and faith-based NGOs with consultative status at the Economic and Social Council of the United Nations are aware of this state of affairs, they nevertheless cooperate with states and within the inter-state system in the framework of ethical and moral influence, and less from the perspective of opposition that advocacy organisations and social movements are inclined to adopt. A feature of this issue of religious actors in international relations is the cooperation among the religious actors themselves, which leads to inter-religious dialogue. In short, a new form of cooperative action in favour of the climate cause is being institutionalised around international cooperation characterised by multi-level governance. The question remains as to how such action can be implemented and whether it can lead to effective climate-oriented mobilisation aimed at reducing GHG emissions at the global level.

Kiel Institute for the World Economy. http://www.economicsejournal.org/economics/discussionpapers/2017-56; Paula J. Posas, "Roles of Religion and Ethics in Addressing Climate Change", *Ethics in Science and Environmental Politics*, 2007, pp. 31–49.

[3] Ludger, Pries, "Les espaces enchevêtrés du tournant global", in A. Caillé & S. Dufoix (eds.), *Le tournant global des sciences sociales*, Paris, La Découverte, 2013, pp.101–114.

Climate action by religious bodies is often articulated in religious institutions' discourses and in their publications as having a doctrinal foundation: it has become a duty for the believer to protect the environment. However, in the space of multilateral negotiations, and especially before the organisation of COP 21, the formulation of their action in terms of moral and values is becoming secularised in order to adopt a universal position on climate justice, which will lead towards the cosmopolitisation of these religious bodies (see Chapter 2).

POSITIONS TAKEN ON THE EVE OF COP 21- PARIS AGREEMENT

The urgency of cooperation on the environment affirmed in religious doctrine is linked to the analysis of religious action to be taken for the sake of the climate and the planet. By asserting an anthropogenic influence on climate change, religious actors reinforce and legitimise the discourse of scientific experts among believers and confirm that climate change is a science-based issue. The scientists are increasingly invited to debate and work with religious actors, who become a force of support for scientists who need believers' influence to advance the cause of climate justice, which means addressing and mitigating climate change.[4] Religious actors know how to encourage new behaviours to benefit the Earth's ecological system among their faith communities and to implement pro-environmental action.[5] Perhaps, it is because of this particular role that former French President François Hollande invited Patriarch Bartholomew I of Constantinople on his official trip to the Philippines to promote COP 21 in Paris.[6]

---

[4] Interviews in Lyon in November 2015 with Nigel Crawhall, who was at that time a member of the Interfaith Liaison Committee (ILC) to the UN Framework Convention on Climate Change (UNFCCC).

[5] The example of *The Islamic Foundation for Ecology & Environmental Sciences* in England and their actions carried out among Muslim believers (http://www.ifees.org.uk/) could also be mentioned. See also the "Roadmap for Congregations, Communities, and Churches for an Economy of Life and Ecological Justice" edited by Rev. Norman Tendis and published by the WCC.

[6] See the following link: https://www.la-croix.com/Urbi-et-Orbi/Actualite/France/Le-patriarche-Bartholomeos-aux-Philippines-avec-Francois-Hollande-2015-02-26-128 5210. According to religious actors present at COP 21 Patriarch Bartholomew was

In international relations, it is essentially the Christian churches that initiated action to make the climate central in religious discourse and promoted actions in the transnational space. Actually, the ecumenical WCC will increasingly become the main voice of the Christian denominations. However, under the papacy of Pope Francis, the Catholic church is now at the forefront of the religious mobilisation to address climate change. Today, religious actors have become a force to transnationalise concerns about the global economic system that both creates wealth and aggravates social inequalities, something which seems to resonate with Liberation Theology. Environmental issues were addressed by Christian leaders in the 1980s and, for example, by the Ecumenical Patriarch Dimitrios, who declared 1 September, which is "the first day of the ecclesiastical year in the Orthodox Church, to be the day of the protection of the natural environment".[7] In 1983, the World Council of Churches (WCC) invited different denominations to join an alliance for protection of the environment. It was at this very moment that, for international religious actors, climate change came to represent "the ultimate threat" and "universal violence against creation and the most vulnerable",[8] especially for the WCC, whose references to climate change by date back to 1988.[9] An inter-religious climate commitment is repeatedly encouraged and was reaffirmed in 2013 during the 10th WCC assembly in Busan, South Korea. In April 2015, the Catholic Church, which is not a member of the WCC, through the Vatican organised an international and inter-religious conference on the climate issue, and announced the publication of a new encyclical by Pope Francis, *Laudato Sí*. However, interfaith dialogue had already been established in 1986 at the level of the official religious leadership for the protection of the environment during the World Wildlife Fund (WWF) international's 25th anniversary celebration

---

scheduled to give a public lecture there, but it was cancelled for security reasons following the terrorist attacks in Paris in November 2015.

[7] G. Kerber, "A Response to Wesley Granberg-Michaelson", in Ernst Conradie & Hilda Koster (eds.), *T&T Clark Handbook of Christian Theology and Climate Change*, London, Bloomsbury, 2020, p. 352.

[8] Interviews with Nigel Crawhall.

[9] G. Kerber, "International advocacy for climate justice", in R. G. Veldman, A. Szasz & R. Haluza-Delay (eds.), *How the World's Religions are Responding to Climate Change. Social Scientific Investigations*, London, Routledge, 2016, p. 279.

in Assisi. During this event, the WWF launched the Network on Conservation and Religion, leading to the formation of the Alliance of Religions and Conservation (ARC).[10] It was Prince Philip, when he was president of WWF, who contributed to invite the world religious leaders of Christianity, Buddhism, Judaism, Islam and Hinduism in Assisi.[11] It is worth mentioning that it was during the same year and few weeks later that Pope John Paul II organised an interfaith event and prayer at Assisi. From 1987, the Community of Sant'Egidio will carry on to promote the "spirit of Assisi" initiated by the Vatican during the annual Meetings of Prayer for Peace. In the 1980s, dialogue and environmental cooperation between denominations and religions represented a new transnational force that international organisations recognised progressively.

As to the context of the multilateral negotiations of the UNFCCC, religious cooperation played an influential role since COP 3 held in Kyoto in 1997, because of different transnational religious networks converging to the same objective: the moral duty to protect the victims of the climate crisis. At Kyoto, the WCC underscored the importance of (inter-)religious cooperation to address the climate issue in its declaration "A Matter of Justice: An Interfaith Statement".[12] Later, COP 12 was held for the first time on the African continent in Nairobi in 2006. An ecumenical and transnational Christian mobilisation of Africa churches calling for international solidarity was organised there for the first time. The Uppsala Manifesto, "Uppsala Interfaith Climate Manifesto 2008", was launched in 2008 at COP 14 in Poznan, an event organised by the WCC to promote interfaith action. It was at the same COP 14 that the Buddhist response to the climate crisis was published. COP 15 in Copenhagen enabled the WCC and Caritas to jointly organise an event meant to exert moral pressure on political decision-makers. Adaptation, a central theme in international negotiations, was finally promoted through the

---

[10] Extract from an online book *Faith for Earth. A Call for Action*, p. 13. « (...) leaders of five of the world's religions—Buddhism, Christianity, Hinduism, Islam and Judaism—presented statements about their traditions' understanding of nature and their religion's values concerning conservation and the environment. Known as the Assisi Declarations, those five statements are regarded as a landmark in religious environmental ethics".

[11] F. M. Khalid, *Signs on the Earth. Islam, Modernity and the Climate Crisis*, Leicestershire, Kube Publishing, 2019, p. 144.

[12] See G. Kerber, "A Response to Wesley Granberg-Michaelson", in Ernst Conradie & Hilda Koster (eds.), *T&T Clark Handbook of Christian Theology and Climate Change*, London, Bloomsbury, 2020, p. 353.

Cancun Adaptation Framework at COP 16 held in Cancun,[13] where religious actors also insisted on the need to take the most vulnerable into account in international public policies addressing climate change. During the Durban COP 17 in 2011, an inter-religious network, WeHaveFaith, rallied and increased the visibility of different churches and religious actors on the international scene. Indeed, it is in South Africa that different South African faith-based actors were recognised by the COP 17 President and UNFCCC executives as an integral part of international climate action.[14] COP 18 in Doha and COP 19 in Warsaw accelerated this drive through interfaith action advancing the cause of addressing climate change, as well as mitigating the risks faced by vulnerable victims of the climate crisis.

In 2013 (COP 19 held in Warsaw), an interfaith liaison committee was established within the COP, which has implications for the UNFCCC, which now has a faith-based interlocutor with whom to collaborate. Faith outreach events are launched, such as #Fastfortheclimate and OurVoices.net. During COP 20 in Lima in 2014, one year before the adoption of the Paris Agreement, national coordination was co-organised by the NGO Religions for Peace and the Peru Inter-religious Council for inter-religious mobilisation. During the same COP 20, a joint statement by the bishops called for an end to the use of fossil fuels. Two days before the United Nations Climate Summit in September 2014, organised by Secretary-General Ban Ki-moon, the Religions for Peace and the WCC co-organised an interfaith climate summit in New York.[15] This resulted in the publication of a declaration on the threats of climate change to be presented to the UN Secretary-General.[16] During 2015 and in view of COP 21, a French inter-religious coordination and the Paris Summit of Conscience for the Climate were organised to which religious dignitaries were invited.[17] For the first time, a collaboration was set up during

---

[13] https://unfccc.int/tools/cancun/adaptation/index.html.

[14] Interview with Nigel Crawhall, who participated at COP 17.

[15] More about the Summit (https://interfaithclimate.org/about-the-summit). Access 2 December 2021. According to the organisers: "One of the objectives of this Interfaith Summit was to convey the faith communities' concerns and proposals to the Secretary General's Climate Summit as part of long term efforts to influence the climate negotiations and the contributions countries bring to the table".

[16] https://interfaithclimate.org/about-the-summit.

[17] Interview with Nigel Crawhall.

the same year between the secular Climate Action Network International (CAN International) and faith-based organisations.[18] Religious leaders have thus become, alongside scientific experts and economic actors, a new cosmopolitan force for advancing international public action in the transnational field of addressing climate change.

For religious leaders, climate action is therefore a theological question linking belief and practice. It is primarily a matter of morality and became urgent in the religious discourse when the climatic disturbances observed by scientific experts as they emerged during the Anthropocene turned into global phenomena. Therefore, religious actors consider necessary a call for an active cooperation, both immediate, short-term and long-term, and in line with the sustainable development objectives. The respective doctrines of each of the religions advocating respect for human life and nature, however, have only recently been based on inter-religious actions with the creation of the interfaith liaison committee within the COP. It is the protection of the poor and the most vulnerable that will become the most pressing cause to be defended in multilateral fora. Indeed, religious actors on the international scene have long anticipated the consequences of the power relations inherent in the international system and which impact on climate negotiations. It is therefore in this specific field of the fight against poverty that we can identify the nature of religious actors' mobilisation on the climate issue.

CLIMATE JUSTICE

Climate justice is gradually becoming a new field of action in line with the social doctrine of the Church: caring for Creation also entails working for social and economic justice for the poorest, which in turn contributes towards a moral vision of peace. Pope Francis's resounding encyclical, *Laudato Si* subtitled "On care for our common home", published in June 2015,[19] illustrated, among other things, the Catholic Church's programmes as initiatives for climate justice. The encyclical advocated ecological action as being at the heart of the Christian faith. In May 2015, the Buddhists' declaration, entitled "The Time to Act is Now: A

---

[18] Interview with Nigel Crawhall.

[19] See more particularly Jean-Dominique Durand, «La papauté et le climat», In P. Martin & S. Sadouni (eds.), Acteurs religieux et changements climatiques, *Histoire, monde & cultures religieuses*, n°40, 2016.

Buddhist Declaration on Climate Change", insisted once again that now was the time for action and expressed the concern "to phase out fossil fuels, to reduce our consumption patterns, and the ethical imperative to act against both the causes and the impacts of climate change, especially on the world's poorest". With regard to Islam, thinkers in recent years have highlighted the urgency of a deeper acceptance of the ecological dimension in achieving the higher objectives of Islamic law (*Mâqasid Ash Shari'a*), knowing that respect for the environment is also at the heart of the doctrine of Islam.[20] During an international symposium organised in Istanbul on 17 and 18 August 2015, religious leaders of Islam, heads of intergovernmental organisations, academics and non-Muslim personalities gathered and the first Islamic declaration on climate change was born. The Islamic declaration, which was also part of an inter-religious international conference, sensitises all citizens to the fact that "If we each offer the best of our respective traditions, we may yet see a way through our difficulties". This international meeting in Istanbul seems to be having repercussions on the international scene and in particular through the creation of foundations and associations for the protection of the environment.[21]

These religious actions to address climate change are increasingly developed within the framework of multilateral negotiations resulting from the UNFCCC and have progressively led, as we have seen, to an institutional recognition by international organisations. For example, the "Declaration of Religious and Spiritual Leaders" for the Conference of the Parties (COP 21) in Paris in December 2015 took up the main lines of the declaration of the Interfaith Summit in New York held on 21 and 22 September 2014.[22] These interfaith actions and discourses will contribute

---

[20] According to the South African Muslim theologian Dr Sheikh Ridwaan Gallant. See his written communication, "The objective (*maqasid*) of the Shari'ah in the protection of the environment", in the context of the convention entitled "Maqasid-Shariah in Twentieth Century", Islamic University of Malaysia, Kuala Lumpur, 8 August 2006. I am grateful to the author for sending me his text. See also S. Sadouni, "L'action interreligieuse pour le climat", *Histoire, monde & cultures religieuses*, n°40, 2016, pp. 111–121.

[21] Ebrahim Rasool, former Premier of the Western Cape province and former South African Ambassador to Washington, DC, attended and participated in the discussions at this international symposium and established the World for All Foundation.

[22] As a preamble, the signatory religious leaders collectively affirm their commitment to climate action: "We", religious leaders, "unite in expressing our deep concern about the consequences of climate change on the earth and its inhabitants, all of whom, according

towards promoting the cause of the poor and climate justice in the debates, which are now leitmotivs for non-state actors in "hybrid forums". IGOs have also joined this religious impetus for acknowledging the moral dimensions of climate change. It is the case of UNEP which in November 2017 launched the Faith for Earth Initiative, of which the mission is to "encourage, empower and engage with faith-based organizations as partners, at all levels, toward achieving the Sustainable Development Goals and fulfilling the 2030 Agenda".[23]

Climate justice stems from the thesis defended by scientific experts that climate risks are unevenly distributed and generally hurt poor and geographically disadvantaged communities, as well as indigenous communities, more severely and at all levels of development.[24] Therefore, climate justice is a matter of human rights in this century and hence a fundamental moral issue, as the former UN Secretary-General, Ban Ki Moon, emphasised on the eve of COP 21: "We are the first generation that can end poverty, and the last generation that can avoid the worst impacts of climate change".[25] Taking into consideration the future—and more specifically unborn generations—in public interest and policymaking is a challenge that has not been sufficiently investigated in political and democratic theory.[26]

Religious and inter-religious action has the advantage of bringing together the forces at play to denounce the advancement of the richest at the expense of the poorest, who are most often compelled to go into exile

---

to our beliefs, are entrusted to our common attention. Climate change is a real threat to life. Life is a precious gift that we have received and must take care of". I am grateful to Guillermo Kerber of the WCC for providing me with a copy of this declaration.

[23] The main partners of UNEP's initiative are the UNFCCC, the Parliament of World's Religions, the World Council of Churches, Brahma Kumaris, Bhumi Global and the Anglican Consultative Office. Together, they "constitute a Multi-faith Working Group on Climate Change". See the following link: https://climateinitiativesplatform.org/index.php/Faith_for_Earth.

[24] (Sachs 2015).

[25] Declaration by Ban Ki Moon UNO Secretary-General "Remarks at dialogue on Democracy, Human Rights, Development, Climate Change and Countering Violent Extremism", 24 August 2015, https://www.un.org/sg/en/content/sg/speeches/2015-08-24/remarks-dialogue-democracy-human-rights-development-climate-change.

[26] (Lidskog & Elander 2010).

to neighbouring countries or, for those who can afford to, distant territories.[27] The struggle for human rights and action to end poverty, which is the number 1 sustainable development goal (SDG) —"no poverty"— is a de facto necessity for religious actors, who remind their co-believers of the theological character of these universal principles in their respective religions. Consequently, the challenge for these inter-religious actors involved in international climate action is to be able to translate the semantics of their religious doctrine into a secular idiom and an ethical language that is universally accessible to believing citizens, certainly, but also to all citizens who subscribe to the public use of reason. The *Laudato Sí* encyclical, the declarations of the Orthodox patriarchs, the Buddhists, the WCC, the Lutheran World Federation statements, the Islamic declaration, among others, all converge in their objective to appeal not only to their own religious communities, but also to all citizens willing to commit themselves to applying their faith and pragmatic reason to protect not only the planet from the consequences of climate change, but also its first victims, the poor.[28]

However, it was the United Nations that took the initiative to recognise the role of religions in discussions on the protection of the planet and to present them as "potentially the most important international civil society movement on climate change in history".[29] The international recognition of religions represents an opportunity for faith-based organisations to further mobilise for climate action and, at the same time, it endows public environmental policies with meaning and significance for believers and practitioners in transnational civil society. The Paris Agreement has formally recognised and integrated non-state actors' actions into the treaty through the concepts of "communities" and "local knowledge

---

[27] See Franck Laczko, Christine Aghazarm (eds.), *Migration, Environment and Climate Change: Assessing the Evidence*, Geneva, International Organization for Migration (IOM), 2009.

[28] (Sadouni 2016).

[29] See excerpts from speeches by UN Secretary-General Ban Ki Moon and Olav Kjørven of the United Nations Development Programme on the occasion of a launch of the organisation's environmental projects, *Alliance of Religions and Conservation* (ARC) in November 2009. As an example, Olav Kjørven made the following remarks: "Potentially the biggest civil society movement on climate change in history" and "the biggest mobilisation of people and communities that we have ever seen on this issue". http://www.arcworld.org/projects.asp?projectID=597.

systems", among others. In the light of the international conference co-organised at the University of Lyon on "Religious Actors and Climate Change", the former Executive Secretary of the UNFCCC, Christiana Figueres, illustrated in her message this intergovernmental organisation's recognition of non-state actors:

> The fact that you are gathered here today to discuss the role of religious leaders facing climate change already speaks loudly to the role of religion as humanity's moral compass. Setting a common direction of how to grow in harmony with each other and the earth has been particularly important to the climate change discourse over the last year. ... 2015 has been an historic year in terms of religious commitments, statements and declarations to support the negotiations and more broadly, to call for humanity to address climate change.

These excerpts from Christiana Figueres's statement demonstrate once again that religious actors represent partners, interlocutors within the United Nations system in the same way as multinational companies are. How can a balance of power be established between multinational corporations' private and financial interests and the moral imperative that religious actors wish to embody? Nicholas Stern, an economist and former World Bank president, who wrote a report on "climate change economics", has, among other things, raised the question of change that is central in the Paris Agreement. By way of a first response to the question of conflict between financial interests and moral action, it is appropriate to look at the dialogue that has been established between scientists and religious experts in order to focus on the potential of religion for supporting global change. An instructive example is the statement by Prof. EO Wilson, a biologist from Harvard University, who recognised that science and religion are the two most powerful forces in the world.[30] He made a plea for the mobilisation of faith communities to save the biodiversity on the planet. The American economist, Jeffrey Sachs, President of the UN Sustainable Development Solutions Network (SDSN) and who served as Special Advisor to UN Secretaries-General Kofi Annan, Ban Ki-moon and António Guterres, had also cooperated with religious leaders.

---

[30] Mary Colwell, "Religion Can Succeed Where the Environment Movement has Failed", *The Guardian*, 23 September 2009, https://www.theguardian.com/commentis free/2009/sep/23/religion-environment-movement.

He has been involved in setting up a teaching programme on the issue of religion and sustainable development that led to the formation of "Ethics in Action", which is a partnership co-hosted by the Chancellor of the Pontifical Academies, the UN Sustainable Development Solutions Network (SDSN), Religions for Peace and the University of Notre Dame. The objective of this consortium is to bring together "global religious and secular ethical leaders to develop a shared moral consensus on the challenges of sustainable development, and to convert this consensus into practical action".[31] All this has implications for the secularisation of global solidarity, which will be discussed later in a section on the Dalai Lama's discourse.

Prevention, Mitigation and Adaptation to Climate Change

Climate action involves the fields of development, education and humanitarian aid in transnational spaces linking the local to the national and international spheres. Indeed, climate change leads to environmental problems that involve behavioural problems at their source. Correcting and modifying behaviours implies educating people to adopt new attitudes; religions have an advantage in this respect as they are able to exert an influence not only through their theology, but also through their educational institutions (schools and universities).[32] These institutions, established in different countries, have a fundamental role to play, since they represent sites for socialising, learning and training that are essential for the circulation of (among other things) new environmental standards. Religions have essentially three educational missions in their climate action, which are also promoted by international environmental organisations and the Paris Agreement: prevention, mitigation and adaptation to climate change. At the December 2019 COP 25 in

---

[31] Anthony Annett, Jeffrey Sachs, Marcelo Sanchez Sorondo, & William Vendley (2017). A Multi-Religious Consensus on the Ethics of Sustainable DEVELOPMENT: reflections of the Ethics in Action Initiative. Economics Discussion Papers, No 2017-56, Kiel Institute for the World Economy. http://www.economicsejournal.org/economics/dis cussionpapers/2017-56.

[32] Mark Morrison, Roderick Duncan, & Kevin Parton, "Religion Does Matter for Climate Change Attitudes and Behavior", *PLoS One*, 10(8), 6 August 2015, https://doi. org/10.1371/journal.pone.0134868.

Madrid, the Catholic Church took the initiative to work on the design of a Global Educational Pact that Pope Francis was to have presented on 14 May 2020, but it was postponed to October because of the COVID-19 pandemic. The network of Catholic Institutes would serve, among other things, to promote respect for nature and humanity in the coming generations.[33]

The Green Pilgrimage and Green Holy Cities initiatives, as well as the Fasting for Climate Justice, also aimed to raise awareness of the climate issue among believers. As an example, each religious denomination carried out its project for the greening of holy cities such as Medina for Muslims, Rome and the Vatican City for Catholics, Amritsar in Punjab for Sikhs, in order to fight against climate change, again in a spirit of coordination and dissemination of information. These initiatives were, for example, implemented jointly by the NGOs Alliance of Religions and Conservation (ARC) and the World Wildlife Fund (WWF international).[34]

In the light of these actions, international organisations tend to accept that faith is no longer simply a matter of belief but of behaviour as well and therefore consider religious actors as partners for sustainable development standards. The low-carbon economy that would make carbon neutrality possible is no longer solely the domain of entrepreneurs and politicians. Civil society's actions and calls for innovation in multi-level governance are increasingly leading to cooperation with religious actors. It is in the highly controversial area of relinquishing the use of fossil fuels[35] that religious actors are increasingly making their mark. In their different declarations, they commonly denounce the increasing use of fossil fuels and advocate within their religious field a sustainable development that must be based on a green economy and the use of renewable energies. The programme "Faith invest" has materialised this new objective as it represents a call of action towards promoting ethical investment

---

[33] We can also mention the networks of schools and the role of Muslim organisations in Indonesia. See Ulil Amri, "From Theology to a Praxis of «eco-jihad»: The Role of Religious Civil Society Organisations in Combating Climate Change in Indonesia", in R. G. Veldman, A. Szasz & R. Haluza-Delay (2014).

[34] (Sadouni 2016).

[35] One example is the UNDP (United Nations Development Programme) report on the importance of reducing fossil fuel emissions to reduce air pollution. "Pursuing the 1,5C° limit. Benefits and Opportunities", 2016 Low Carbon Monitor.

by different faith-based institutions.[36] Religion is certainly about belief, rituals practices and faith, but there is also a business dimension in religion. For example, religious institutions and faiths are considered to own about 8% of the habitable land surface of the earth and about 5% of all commercial forests. By owning an estimated 10% of the world's total financial investment, the business dimension of religion controls the management of assets and investments[37] in line with the issue of disinvesting from companies exploiting fossil fuels that we saw earlier (see Chapter 3).

It is no longer only the countries of the North that are targeted by religious advocacy to end the exploitation and use of fossil fuels, but also China and India, among others. These countries are both becoming important players in the race for energy resources. A new geopolitics of mineral resources is taking shape, as can be observed with the new military defence policies in the maritime space[38]; 90% of manufactured production transits along maritime routes, not to mention oil transport. New American and even Chinese military bases are being built in Africa and in the Gulf countries in order to secure the maritime routes of the northeastern Indian Ocean. As in the case of the Artic and the project of a Northern Route for the transit of commercial goods (Chapter 3), religious actors are becoming aware that this geopolitics is shaping our new international system and have been concerned about the absence of public policies aimed at ending the exploitation of fossil fuels. For example, the signatories of the Islamic Declaration on Climate Change, on the eve of COP 21, urged oil-producing states and affluent countries to reduce

---

[36] See FaithInvest which has for mission "to accelerate and broaden faith-consistent, values-driven investing by empowering faith groups to invest in line with their values. We do so by providing a membership NETWORK for faith-based investors, a SOURCE of education, exchange and collaboration, a PLATFORM for investment ideas, opportunities and concepts, and a VOICE for the faiths and values-driven investors". https://www.faithinvest.org/our-mission.

[37] See publication of the Alliance of Religions and Conservation compiled by Martin Palmer and Pippa Moss and entitled "The ZUG Guidelines for Faith-Consistent Investment. Faith in Finance. What Do You Do with Wealth to Make a Better Planet?", 2017, pp. 5–6.

[38] Anthony Giddens, *The Politics of Climate Change*, Cambridge, Polity Press, 2011.

their GHG emissions as early as possible.[39] They go further by emphasising, like the Buddhists' declaration, the ethics and moral obligation towards humanity and the divine: "the same fossil fuels that helped us achieve most of the prosperity we see today are the main cause of climate change. Excessive pollution from fossil fuels threatens to destroy the gifts bestowed on us by God – gifts such as a functioning climate, healthy air to breathe, regular seasons, and living oceans. But our attitude to these gifts has been short-sighted, and we have abused them. What will future generations say of us, who leave them a degraded planet as our legacy? How will we face our Lord and Creator?".

These same signatories of the "Islamic declaration on global climate change" asked the oil-producing states, most of which, it should be recalled, are part of the Muslim world, as well as "well-off nations" to:

- Provide generous financial and technical support to the less well-off to achieve a phase-out of greenhouse gasses as early as possible;
- Recognise the moral obligation to reduce consumption so that the poor may benefit from what is left of the earth's non-renewable resources;
- Stay within the "2 degree" limit, or, preferably, within the "1.5 degree" limit, bearing in mind that two-thirds of the earth's proven fossil fuel reserves remain in the ground;
- Re-focus their concerns from unethical profit from the environment, to preserving it and elevating the condition of the world's poor;
- Invest in the creation of a green economy.[40]

A similar recent statement, "A Joint statement by national Muslim organisations in the United Kingdom & Ireland", has called on the world leaders gathered for the COP 26 conference in Glasgow to commit, among others, to the following:

- End to all use of public money to subsidise fossil fuels.

---

[39] See the following links: https://unfccc.int/fr/news/declaration-islamique-sur-les-changements-climatiques; http://www.climatenetwork.org/category/tags/islamic-climate-declaration.

[40] https://www.ifees.org.uk/wp-content/uploads/2020/01/climate_declaratio nmmwb.pdf.

- Divest from fossil fuels and further commit to a total greening of energy sources.
- Access new and additional sources of finance to address climate-related loss and damage.

These main points are again commonly shared by all religious actors engaged in the mitigation of global warming and are related to measures and policies that are recommended in the Paris Agreement. However, with non-state actors' declarations ahead of COP 26, it is now clearly stated that the 1.5 degree limit is the one that must be targeted by the parties of the UNFCCC. Scientific knowledge and expertise assert that in order to remain within the 1.5 °C limit, emissions must be reduced by about 45% by 2030 and coal must be phased out. Consumption of all fossil fuels must be massively reduced, and fossil fuel subsidies must end. During COP 26 at Glasgow, some progress was made on non-renewable energy and as asserted by the WCC in its statement: "an agreement by more than 40 countries—including major coal-users such as Poland, Vietnam and Chile—to shift away from coal, one of the biggest generators of CO2 emissions; the creation by 11 countries of the Beyond Oil and Gas Alliance (BOGA), including some sub-national authorities, to set an end date for national oil and gas exploration and extraction".[41] The event most circulated by the media, remains, however, the bilateral US-China agreement to work together on cutting greenhouse gas emissions over the next decade. What was also agreed, and it was part of the rule book of the Paris Agreement, is the period of reviewing the Nationally Determined Commitments of the Parties. The Paris Agreement required revision of NDCs every 5 years, while the COP 26 outcome mandate annual reviews. Annual revision of these commitments is considered to be the minimum condition for maintaining any hope of remaining within the 1.5 °C threshold.

Through these different categories of international public action, the economic and political challenges are considered as important by religious actors engaged in the protection of the environment. By advocating for climate justice for the poorest, they also promote greater religious

---

[41] Statement on the outcome of COP 26 by the WCC Executive Committee, November 2021, https://www.oikoumene.org/resources/documents/statement-on-the-outcome-of-cop26.

tolerance at the same time. This rationale is indeed at the heart of religious actors' discourse, as they insist on the importance of solidarity on the international scene; it is indeed important for them that political, economic and cultural boundaries must become more permeable for the sake of the protection of quality of life for today's—but also of tomorrow's—humans and other living species. For UNEP's Faith for Earth director, even if we have the technology and finance for achieving the objectives of climate mitigation, the political will is fundamental: "We are in a race against time that will require political will, innovation, inclusion, tolerance, values and ethics, financing, and partnerships. (...) The world has the scientific understanding, the technological capacity, and the financial means to do this".[42] Along with the necessary financial and technical capacity, climate action and mitigation policies also need ethical capabilities such as tolerance and solidarity.

From these different positions taken by international religious actors on climate change, we can put forward the idea that we have entered a new era of sustainable development which includes religion.[43] As Anthony Giddens points out,[44] it is difficult for human beings to project themselves into the future or to consider their health and lifestyle twenty years in advance in order to change the situation for a beneficial result in the years to come. The future is difficult to grasp, but it exists even in its uncertain and even anxiety-provoking nature. At multi-level governance, religious actors have sought to intervene in this debate around the issue of climate and, more broadly, the future of humanity and the planet. This was notably the case, as we saw, at a conference organised at the Vatican on 28 April 2015, which illustrates the modern moral order and which was supported by the Pontifical Academy of Sciences and Social Sciences, the UN's SDSN (Sustainable Development Solutions Network) and the NGO Religions for Peace, whose office is located at the United Nations in New York. The conference was entitled "Protect the Earth, Dignify Humanity: The Moral Dimensions of Climate Change and Sustainable

---

[42] Iyad Abumoghli, Director of Faith for Earth Strategic Engagement with Faith-based Organizations Executive Office United Nations Environment Programme Nairobi, Kenya. In United Nations Environment Programme and Parliament of the World's Religions (2020), *Faith for Earth: A Call for Action*, UNEP, Nairobi. https://wedocs.unep.org/bitstream/handle/20.500.11822/33991/FECA.pdf?sequence=1&isAllowed=y.

[43] Charles Taylor, *A Secular Age*, Harvard University Press, 2007.

[44] Giddens (2011).

Development" and was attended by UN Secretary-General Ban Ki Moon and 60 religious, scientific and academic leaders. Punctuated by debates, that day was also intended, according to Bishop Sanchez Sorondo— Chancellor of the Pontifical Academy of Sciences and Social Sciences—to enable the Pope to influence the multilateral debates and negotiations to be held in November 2015 during COP 21 in Paris.[45] Bishop Sorondo stressed the importance of raising awareness of the climate issue and the "tragedy of social exclusion". A similar international event was organised in 2021 with a different outcome in the form of an appeal. The meeting on "Faith and Science: Towards COP26", promoted by the Embassies of Great Britain and Italy to the Holy See, together with the Holy See, was held once again at the Vatican on 4 October 2021. It brought together about 40 faith leaders of the world's major religions and scientists from 20 countries.[46] During the meeting, an appeal mentioned the expectations of the faith community for COP 26 and their commitment to action and was addressed to the political decision-makers and participants gathered in COP 26. It was handed by Pope Francis to Alok Kumar Sharma, president of COP 26, and Luigi Di Maio, Italian Minister of Foreign Affairs and International Cooperation. This international event was mostly intended to raise ambitions with regard to what can be achieved by COP 26. However, different organisations from international civil society, including religious institutions, have since expressed their ongoing disappointment with the inadequate outcomes of COP 26.

So far, science and religion have come together at the international level to address the issue of climate change. The two are no longer opposed in the pursuit of the common good and this common cause for the climate has revealed the limits of a wholly secular reading of international relations, since religion, international organisations and science are now aligned in the fight against global warming. In this regard, I would like to quote the words of the Dalai Lama, leader of Tibetan Buddhism, which explain the secular approach adopted by faith-based actors in dealing with sustainable development. In his dialogue with Stéphane Hessel, resistance fighter, French diplomat and observer when

---

[45] See, in particular, his comments in a press article in the *National Catholic Reporter*: https://www.ncronline.org/news/vatican/un-leader-asks-francis-help-addressing-climate-change.

[46] https://www.reuters.com/world/europe/vatican-hopes-its-pre-cop26-climate-event-will-raise-stakes-glasgow-2021-10-03/ (Access 03/12/2021).

the Universal Declaration of Human Rights was issued in1948, he relates how his faith informs his positioning on the international scene and in defence of the environment:

> I am a Buddhist monk, indeed, a man of faith, and as such I have made harmony between religions my commitment. But when I introduce myself, I say: I am one of the seven billion beings that populate the planet and, in this human body, I have set myself the task of taking care of humanity. Not of a nation, not of a government but of humanity in the broadest sense, and beyond that, of the planet we share with animals, plants, and which is our only home.[47]

He goes on to comment on actors' interdependence and the need for secular cooperation:

> All religions have their own unique beauty and we must be respectful of them. But if we are to reach a universal level, we must place ourselves on another level, the level of a secular ethic. Secular does not mean disrespect for religion. Secular ethics respects all religions and equally respects non-believers, who have the right to continue not to believe. ... In the Universal Declaration of Human Rights, there is no distinction between this or that religion, between one nation and another. It is about all of humanity.

What can we conclude from this? That there is a re-enchantment of international reality illustrated by religious cosmopolitanism. It is part of a secularised approach that is desired and not imposed on religious actors. Nevertheless, the Dalai Lama's speech, which illustrates the nature of religious actors' environmental action, should not blind us to this fact: financing is a central and decisive issue in the interdependence of international policies aimed at protecting the planet. The Green Fund, which is related to the Paris Agreement in Article 9 mentioning "developed country Parties shall provide financial resources to assist developing country Parties with respect to both mitigation and adaptation in continuation of their existing obligations under the Convention", is the focus of intense discussions. According to a study by the Berkley Center for Religion, Peace & World Affairs, religious actors do not seem to be taking an

---

[47] Our translation from French to English. Dalaï-Lama, Stéphane Hessel, *Déclarons la paix ! Pour un progrès de l'esprit*, Indigène Publishers, 2012, pp. 10–12.

active part yet in discussions.[48] Nevertheless, we can cite in this regard the international confessional network "WeHaveFaith. Act now for climate justice", which notably published a recommendation from African faith leaders on the occasion of COP 18. These leaders cited the Green Fund of 100 billion dollars per year by 2020, meant to prioritise the interests of poor and vulnerable countries. They also insisted on the taxation of multinational firms.[49] However, green values and ethics are not enough without the political will and strong public policies that can encourage global change in favour of efficient environmental governance.[50] Participants in the *Ethics in Action* initiative recommend that, in order to advance sustainable development, for example, it is necessary to "tax the wealth held in tax havens at a rate of up to 1 percent, raising as much as $200 billion per year", but also to "urge all wealthy countries to honor the commitment to 0.7 percent of GDP in Official Development Aid (ODA). This currently stands at about 0.3 percent of GDP in the rich countries, a shortfall of about $200 billion a year".[51] These proposals and the faith-based organisations' investment strategies to fight global warming tend to reinforce religious capabilities in the transnational field of climate action or the transnational climate field.

---

[48] Shaun, Casey and Micah, Musser, "Religious Actors and Climate Change: From Advocacy to Action", White Paper, November 2018, https://berkleycenter.georgetown.edu/publications/religious-actors-and-climate-change-from-advocacy-to-action.

[49] I am quoting excerpts from this four-page brochure that I obtained in South Africa: "African governments need to self-finance their climate adaptation and mitigation strategies, drawing on the diverse resources through domestic resource mobilisation from the State. These resources can be obtained from progressive tax systems such as increasing the tax from multinational corporations and the wealthy, financial transaction taxes, and regulation on capital flows, amongst others". See also the following document "WeHave-Faith act now for climate justice", http://safcei.org/wp-content/uploads/2015/06/We-have-faith.pdf.

[50] R. Lidskog & I. Elander consider that "these institutions must include strong decision-making structures, binding agreements and rules, structures for distributing accountability and efficient systems of legal sanctions. But where do we find such structures?", (Lidskog & Elander 2010: 38).

[51] Anthony Annett, Jeffrey Sachs, Marcelo Sanchez Sorondo, & William Vendley (2017). A Multi-Religious Consensus on the Ethics of Sustainable Development: Reflections of the Ethics in Action Initiative. Economics Discussion Papers, No 2017-56, Kiel Institute for the World Economy. http://www.economics-ejournal.org/economics/discussionpapers/2017-56.

CHAPTER 5

Climate Action, Religion and Civil Society in South Africa

An analysis of the national level that impacts on the discourses and actions of transnational religious actors engaged in the climate cause remains essential in the study of glocal climate politics and the transnational field of climate action. Climate action in the local context is also the result of the "boomerang effect" described by Keck and Sikking[1] and is part of internationalising the climate agenda. The case of South Africa enables us to shed light on the relations between religion, society, the environment/climate and politics.

For South Africa, the study of the local as embodied in civil society takes place in a political context marked by the accession of the African National Congress (ANC) to power and government of the newly democratic state since 1994. The relationship between religion and the political sphere will be analysed by examining the mutual influence that they exert on the action of a multi-faith NGO, SAFCEI (Southern African Faith Communities' Environment Institute), which is dedicated to the protection of the environment. The role of international organisations such as UNDP (United Nations Development Programme) in the emergence of SAFCEI is also an aspect that cannot be neglected in the analysis

---

[1] Margaret E. Keck & Kathryn Sikkink, *Activists Beyond Borders: Advocacy Networks in International Politics*, Ithaca, NY, Cornell University Press, 1998.

© The Author(s), under exclusive license to Springer Nature Switzerland AG 2022
S. Sadouni, *Religious Transnationalism and Climate Change*,
Human Rights Interventions,
https://doi.org/10.1007/978-3-031-10610-1_5

of the transnational climate field. The aim in this chapter is to understand the local and community forms of climate action based on the notion of an eco-congregation, which reflects the community formation process characterised by, among other things, inter-religious dialogue and environmental action. In exploring the case of South African society, I will draw on the work of Paulo Freire,[2] who developed the concept of conscientisation (awareness building) related to environmental issues as well as the notion of the development community. Freire's views will enable us to identify the main characteristics of SAFCEI, which places climate justice and awareness of one's own condition at the centre of its eco-congregationalist activities in order to act more effectively.

SAFCEI seeks to embody another way of acting for sustainable development in comparison to that of the faith-based NGO, Gift of the Givers. The latter is well-known in South Africa and undertakes humanitarian and emergency work. The moral economy of development embodied by SAFCEI, however, translates into climate change mitigation and adaptation actions aimed at reducing the impact of the consequences of climate change on the most vulnerable populations before the humanitarian response.

Communication is essential for the establishment of this pro-environmental community and for eco-congregations to influence society to act to address climate change. Habermas considers communication activities to be society's original constitutive element, the one that can help define social norms, values and roles that are essential in the creation of a society.[3] For Habermas, the state is weakened if it does not engage in appropriate communicational actions and apply the axioms relating to social solidarity, which are indispensable for the state's cohesion and permanence. This is also what Durkheim found in his work on the subject of anomie within society and what is needed to build social ties. But Habermas insists much more on the fact that the rule of law can neither be achieved nor sustained without "radical democracy". The new South Africa hastened to adopt radical democratic principles at its inception, but some consider this condition to be primarily a "deferred democracy" that

---

[2] P. Freire, *Pedagogy of the Oppressed*, Harmondsworth, Penguin, 1972; P. Freire, *The Politics of Education: Culture, Power and Liberation*, London, Macmillan, 1985; P. Freire, *Pedagogy of Freedom: Ethics, Democracy and Civic Courage*, Oxford, Rowman & Littlefield, 1998.

[3] J. Habermas, *Droit et Démocratie. Entre faits et normes*, Paris, Gallimard, 1997.

has failed to meet the radical expectations of its most vulnerable populations. I will return to this last point later in order to understand the
emergence of faith-based development and climate NGOs in this context
of "deferred democracy".[4]

As for the concept of an eco-congregation embodied by SAFCEI,
among others, I would like to come back to its inter-religious dimension because, as we have seen, the climate action is not the business of
one religion alone, but rather the business of all for all. It is therefore
appropriate to begin the analysis of inter-religious relations in South Africa
through a study of the ANC, which has contributed most to the institutionalisation of a dialogue among religions in the new South African
political field. Interfaith dialogue has its preconditions. These include
easing internal tensions, i.e. between different intra-faith groups. Does
the ANC-dominated state play an influential role in these internal negotiations? I will focus on South Africa's state actions and specifically on
the ANC's strategy of homogenising religious representation through
working cooperatively with different denominations. To this end, I adopt
the following hypothesis: this initiative of cooperation of the state and
social dialogue between religions, which is not new in the history of
South African society, will contribute to the establishment of confessional environmental NGOs such as SAFCEI in a democratic context.
This chapter will posit that the state does matter and plays an important
role which, of course, explains local politics, but also influences intergovernmental organisations' stance towards religions and religious actors on
the international scene (see Chapter 3).

African National Congress (ANC):
Dialogue of Religions and Public Policy

In South Africa, 80% of the population identifies with a religion, or
is attached to a religious community or church.[5] In the light of this
majority attachment to religion, dialogue between religions is becoming
a key issue to sustain social cohesion in post-apartheid South Africa. Is

---

[4] See more particularly the biography of the former South African President, Thabo
Mbeki: Mark Gevisser, *Thabo Mbeki. The Dream Deferred*, Johannesburg, Jonathan Ball,
2007.

[5] See in particular https://www.firstthings.com/article/1990/10/religion-and-the-
new-south-africa.

the state driving such engagement in South Africa? Or should we rather focus on its main representative, the ANC? And if so, what is the ANC's role in supporting inter-religious dialogue? Has the ANC politicised and secularised religions in the new South Africa?

Religion in South Africa played a central role in the institutionalisation of racial segregation, particularly through the Dutch Reformed Church (DRC), an Afrikaner variant of Calvinism. But religion (including Afrikaner Calvinism) was also the driving force in the struggle against apartheid, illustrating religious actors' capacity to affirm or oppose apartheid. From the 1980s, different faiths joined forces to resist apartheid. While civil society participated in inter-religious actions during the apartheid period, what is the situation since democratisation? It is the ANC-dominated state that played a role in institutionalising inter-religious dialogue. In fact, the ANC tried to organise an inter-religious dialogue that the United Democratic Front (UDF), an anti-apartheid social movement, had incarnated before in the 1980s through the leadership of, among others, Desmond Tutu. However, questions need to be asked: Was this initiative a new public policy being pursued by the ANC? Or did it rather represent a political recuperation of the ANC? Or was this promotion of interfaith dialogue a tradition within the ANC? I will focus the analysis on the last question. For it is necessary to understand from a socio-historical perspective the influence of the religious dimension within this political liberation movement that has now been a central political party in the country for more than 25 years, and is well-known on the African continent.[6]

The influence of the religious sphere is observable in the ANC's history, particularly when one takes into account the biographies of the founders of the ANC, who belonged to South African Christian churches. It was with Nelson Mandela's democratic presidency that the religious and more particularly the inter-religious organisations such as the National Religious Leaders Forum affirmed the links between religion and ANC politics. Mandela is, indeed, the one who contributed greatly to the institutionalisation of a platform for religious dialogue in South

---

[6] S. Booysen, *The African National Congress and the Regeneration of Political Power*, Johannesburg, Wits University Press, 2011; A. Lissoni, J. Soske, N. Erlank, N. Nieftago-dien, & O. Badsha (eds.), *One Hundred Years of the ANC: Debating Liberation Histories Today*, Johannesburg, WUP, 2012.

African politics. But before highlighting the different stages of this institu-tionalisation, it is necessary to examine from a socio-historical perspective the presence of religion in the African political field and more particularly within the ANC.

In order to understand the relationship between religion and the ANC, it is first necessary to look at Christianity[7] and more specifically the mission schools in South Africa[8] from a socio-historical perspec-tive. Many of the ANC's key leaders, from its founding in 1912 to the generation of Nelson Mandela and Oliver Tambo, were the products of these mission schools, where they received their academic and reli-gious training.[9] Despite the poor quality of primary education provided in the vast majority of these schools, there was a small group of elite secondary schools where ANC leaders were trained. These included the very large schools at Lovedale and Healdtown in the Eastern Cape and a few others in the Transvaal, such as St. Peter's in Johannesburg. There were also Wellington, Kilnerton, Clarkesbury (where Mandela studied), Tigerkloof and the American Board of Missions school in Amanzimtoti, Natal. These schools tended to be run by English or Scottish mission-aries; they often had good teachers who were British university graduates and who helped to train students to a high intellectual level. Despite their paternalistic approach, they often felt impelled to convey aspirations for social progress that were strongly opposed by segregationists. This was the main reason why the apartheid government closed these schools in the 1950s. Fort Hare University was central to the missionaries' educa-tional project and to the education not only of South African political

---

[7] Adrian, Hastings, *A World History of Christianity*, Eerdmans, 2000; see also by the same author *African Christianity*, Seabury Pr, 1977.

[8] See in particular Natasha Erlank's work: Natasha Erlank, "Re-examining Initial Encounters Between Christian Missionaries and the Xhosa, 1820–1850: the Scottish Case", *Kleio*, 31 (1), 1999, pp. 6–32.

[9] Biography of Sol Plaatje by Brian Willan, *Sol Plaatje: South African Nationalist, 1876–1932*, Johannesburg, 1984; see also the biographies of John Dube by Heather Hughes, *The First President: A Life of John L. Dube, Founding President of the ANC*, Jacana Media, 2011; of A.B. Xuma by Steven Gish, Alfred B. Xuma: African, American, South African, New York, New York University Press, 2000; and articles published on Modiri Molema by Jane Starfield, "A Dance with the Empire: Modiri Molema's Glasgow Years, 1914–1921", *Journal of Southern African Studies*, 27 (3), 2001, pp. 479–503; Jane Starfield, "A Member of the Race': Dr Modiri Molema's Intellectual Engagement with the Popular History of South Africa, 1912–1921", *South African historical journal*, 64 (3), 2012, pp. 434–449.

leaders, but also of other African leaders such as Robert Mugabe (the first president of Zimbabwe), Seretse Khama (the first president of Botswana), Julius Nyerere (the first president of Tanzania) and Kenneth Kaunda (the first president of Zambia). These schools were attached to denominational churches in England or Scotland: Methodist, Wesleyan, Anglican, Congregationalist or Presbyterian.[10]

This religious socialisation was an important influence on the leadership of the African political elite.[11] Oliver Tambo, for example, was known to be an Anglican believer who regularly attended mass. Few key ANC leaders chose to change their mainstream Christian denomination to join Zionist or independent churches. Even those who did become secular or even Marxist were still influenced by a Christian missionary culture. Missionary schools were also important in translating scripture into African languages. Religious proselytising was thus part of the development of printing in African languages, a first step towards the development of an African political press.[12] Missionary schools thus unwittingly participated in linking nationalism and printing, as Benedict Anderson[13] had analysed the process. The character of Albert Luthuli is also pertinent in understanding the influence of the religious sphere in the history of the ANC. The first Nobel Peace Prize winner from the African continent and ANC president from 1952 to 1967, Luthuli publicly evinced his religious beliefs and continued to generate debate in Southern Africa about his possible rejection of political violence as

---

[10] I am grateful to Jonathan Hyslop, Professor at the Colgate University (USA), historian, sociologist and a specialist on South Africa for his information on the topic.

[11] See in particular Z.K. Matthews, *Freedom for My People. The Autobiography of Z.K. Matthews: Southern Africa 1901 to 1968* (edited by M. Wilson), Cape Town, David Philip, 1981; the first two chapters of the autobiography of Mandela: N. Mandela, *Un long chemin vers la liberté*, Paris, Fayard, 1995; Luli Callinicos, *Oliver Tambo: His Life and Legacy: 1917–1993*, Franciscan Academic Press, 2019.

[12] Isabel Hofmeyr, *The Portable Bunyan. A Transnational History of The Pilgrim's Progress*, Johannesburg, Wits University Press, 2004.

[13] Benedict Anderson, *L'imaginaire national. Réflexions sur l'origine et l'essor du nationalisme*, Paris, La Découverte, 1996 (translation). See also regarding the African nationalism: Andre Odendaal, *Vukani Bantu!: The Beginnings of Black Protest in South Africa*, Cape Town, D. Philip, 1984.

president of the political organisation.[14] Peter Limb's work[15] provides valuable insights into the movement, but does not sufficiently take into account the ANC founders' accommodation of British imperial politics and their socialisation into the values of the missionary world.[16] This issue of religion and politics in South Africa has been addressed in part by scholars in the Department of Religious Studies at the University of Cape Town, including the work of John de Gruchy, Charles Villa-Vicencio and David Chidester.[17] The political liberation movements were clearly involved in the formation of the post-apartheid state and the South African political field dominated by the ANC, as a movement and political party. Because the presence of religion within the ANC is a social component that cannot be ignored, we therefore need to understand the nature of the relationships between religion and politics in order to better understand the history of South African politics.

Mandela is, as we have seen, the one who initiated the creation of the National Religious Leaders Forum and reorganised church-state relations in South Africa.[18] These relations are essentially based on cooperation, with visible changes that became clear when religious actors publicly criticised Jacob Zuma and his administration during his second presidential

---

[14] Albert Luthuli, *Let My People Go: An Autobiography*, HarperCollins, 1987; see also Scott Couper, *Albert Luthuli. Bound by Faith*, Pietermaritzburg, University of KwaZulu-Natal Press, 2010.

[15] Peter Limb, *The ANC's Early Years: Nation, Class and Place in South Africa Before 1940*, Pretoria, UNISA Press, 2010.

[16] See also Gail M. Gerhart, Thomas Karis, Gwendolen Carter, *From Protest to Challenge: A Documentary History of African Politics in South Africa, 1882–1964*, Hoover Inst Pr, 1977.

[17] John De Gruchy, *The Churches Struggle*, Minneapolis, Fortress Press, 2004; M. Prozesky & J. De Gruchy, *Living Faiths in South Africa*, London, Hurst & Company, 1995; Charles Villa-Vicencio, *Trapped In Apartheid: A Socio-Theological History of the English-Speaking Churches*, Maryknoll, Orbis Books, 1988; C. Villa-Vicencio, *South African Leaders on Religion and Politics*, Berkeley, University of California Press, 1996; C. Villa-Vicencio, *Civil Disobedience And Beyond: Law, Resistance and Religion in South Africa*, Ann Arbor, UMI2000; David Chidester, *Religions of South Africa*, London, Routledge, 1992; David Chidester, Abdulkader Tayob, Wolfram Weisse, *Religion, Politics, and Identity in a Changing South Africa*, Münster, Waxmann, 2004.

[18] Raymond Simangaliso Kumalo, "Facts and Faction: The Development of Church and State Relations in Democratic South Africa from 1994–2012", *Church State*, 56 (4), 2014, pp. 627–643; Tracy Kuperus, *State, Civil Society and Apartheid in South Africa: An Examination of Dutch Reformed Church-State Relations*, Houndmills, Basingstoke: Macmillan and New York: St. Martin's Press, 1999.

term. We will not pursue this last point here, but rather focus on the historical process of cooperation between religious organisations and the state. This will lead to a better understanding of religious governance mechanisms in a society marked by constitutionally guaranteed religious freedom.

Nevertheless, the transnational dimension remains important in understanding the relationship between society and religion (see Chapter 2). Transnational mobility was important in building an inter-religious platform for the struggle against apartheid in South Africa. The call for transnational religious solidarity has served the wider struggle for justice and respect for human rights.

Gradually, inter-religious dialogue became institutionalised in the new South Africa through the integration of religious leaders of different traditions into the democratisation process; this include those who cooperated in achieving the objective of a political transformation that could finally be enshrined in the country's new constitution. The recognition by the new democratic state of the strength of the religious sphere is reflected in particular by Mandela's appointment of Desmond Tutu to chair the Truth and Reconciliation Commission. Mandela was convinced that the religious establishment in South African society had an essential role to play in the country's democratisation. This was followed by the creation of the Advisory Board for Religious Broadcasting and the National Religious Leaders Forum (NRLF). Since the end of apartheid, the state has taken charge of the institutionalisation of inter-religious affairs through the creation of various organisations that can be considered parastatal. This has become an important issue in the religious public policy of the ruling ANC.

Religious organisations represented in the NRLF and later in the National Interfaith Council of South Africa were invited by political authorities to promote the ideal of unity by legitimising the nation-building programme, nevertheless led by the ANC. Take the example of the current President, Cyril Ramaphosa; in his speech at a meeting with religious leaders—the National Religious Leaders Council and the National Interfaith Council of South Africa—and members of the government, he emphasised the common values that monotheistic religions share with the country's constitutional values.[19]

---

[19] See   https://www.gov.za/speeches/president-cyril-ramaphosa-interfaith-leaders-mee ting-10-apr-2019-0000.

While Mandela played a role in the dialogue not only among religions but also between the state and religious actors, the question is whether the calls for an eco-congregation such as embodied by SAFCEI as a multi-faith-based NGO emerged from society only, or jointly from society and the state, or even more significantly from society, state and international organisations. The trajectory of SAFCEI illustrates the last tripartite dimension which integrates civil society, the state and international institutions such as UNDP, without denying the existence of tensions and the need for negotiations with the state. Faith-based NGOs in South African civil society have historically maintained links with the ANC in its struggle against apartheid, but in democratic times, they have developed a more critical approach to the ANC, as shown by the case of SAFCEI in the field of environmental protection.

SAFCEI: COOPERATION, TENSIONS AND RECONCILIATION BETWEEN THE ENVIRONMENTAL FAITH-BASED NGO SECTOR AND THE STATE

Faith-based NGOs in South Africa and more broadly in Southern Africa have been able to develop an inter-religious dialogue in the humanitarian field, particularly through cooperation in the implementation of AIDS-prevention programmes.[20] However, it is in the field of environmental protection that the most successful forms of inter-religious action can be observed, and more specifically those aimed at combating the social consequences of climate change. Although SAFCEI does not identify itself as an inter-religious NGO,[21] its activities are based exclusively on the joint initiatives of different religious actors. On its website, SAFCEI prefers to use the term "multi-religious" to describe this feature[22]:

Multi-faith dialogue based on equity, justice, and mutual respect for the Earth, is a way we can build a sustainable future for all. A multi-faith

---

[20] S. Sadouni, «Humanisme spirituel et ONG islamiques en Afrique du Sud», *Afrique Contemporaine*, n°231, 2009, pp. 157-170.

[21] Interview with Bishop Geoff Davies, founder of SAFCEI, 2 December 2021.

[22] See the organisation's website at https://safcei.org/about-us/.

approach raises awareness about the diverse traditions that help people to grow spiritually through a deeper connection with creation.[23]

Established in 2005 as a multi-faith organisation, SAFCEI supports religious leaders and their respective communities in Southern Africa to raise awareness of climate action, eco-justice and sustainable living. Because of the need to act together, SAFCEI carries out activities specific to an eco-congregation, which the organisation defines as "all people of faith caring for life's sacred community". This definition, which also alludes to the need for respect for living together, community life and tolerance as principles that are indispensable for reforming action, at the same time reveals SAFCEI's socio-environmental and political objectives. Any pro-environmental mobilisation must therefore be rooted in the construction of a plural community that strengthen unifying forces and aspirations for a better world. The notion of sacred unity implicit in the term of an eco-congregation thus represents a political idea. The community must also, according to Freire, identify its needs and develop an awareness of the challenges facing society.

The cooperation of religious actors in climate action represents a new form of religious dialogue: beyond the protection of the planet, it also aims at social justice, collective security and peace that contribute to structure their moral economy. This is because, as we have seen, climate change has consequences in terms of pollution, poverty, sustainable development, the management of natural resources as well as the flow of refugees. It is therefore appropriate here to reflect on the modalities of this inter-religious action for the climate, which thus represents a higher stage of inter-religious dialogue based on moral values. Indeed, dialogue is above all a means of discussing differences and a tool for reaching agreement between various opposing or conflicting parties. However, in addressing climate action, all religious actors agree that climate change is induced by human activities and that, consequently, the environmental emergency demands the dropping of confessional boundaries for the sake of global action to protect the planet and its common goods.[24] It is worth mentioning the role of UNDP in their suggestion to include all of South Africa's main faiths (Christianity being the overall majority, but also

---

[23] https://safcei.org/project/multi-faith/.

[24] (Sadouni 2016).

Bahai, Hindu, Muslim, Buddhist, African Traditional Religion and Jewish communities)[25] at the founding SAFCEI which started as an ecumenical initiative endorsed by the South African Council of Churches. The inter-religious issue can become an intra-religious matter when it comes to convincing members of one's own as well as different faith groups of the need to open up to the Other, or even of the existence of human-induced global warming.

The future of the planet which is described as being "everyone's concern" cannot be negotiated within a communitarian or individual-istic approach: it requires cosmopolitical approach, i.e. the relationship to otherness and common action for the protection of the common goods of every human inhabitant of the planet at present and in the future. However, acting with others does not imply that all members of one's religious community would agree with such cooperation. However, the resurgence of denominations and currents within the same religious field makes it difficult to be acknowledged as a representative faith actor engaged in inter-religious action. Religious actors studied here are not necessarily considered as representatives of the faith group to which they belong. Other members of their faith group can disagree or criticise their interfaith action. The path of ecumenism may offer a remedy without, however, silencing the dissension that characterises all social and religious fields. In South Africa, it is the joint impact of religious citizenship and community bonds that has shaped the eco-congregation; this has benefited the SAFCEI and served its "multi-faith" dimension.

The Moral Economy of Development, the Neoliberal Context and Religious Citizenship

In South Africa, faith-based associations and NGOs in the fields of devel-opment and humanitarian aid are part of socio-political trajectories that are essentially conducive to promoting living together and sustaining a citizen ethic of sharing. The passage to faith-based NGOs' nationalisa-tion implies a change in religious activism. What are the changes within the field of activism brought by actors involved in the field of sustain-able development and climate change? The increasing professionalisation

---

[25] See Bishop Geoff Davies, "SAFCEI (Southern African Faith Communities' Envi-ronment Institute)" http://archive.sciendo.com/ANV/anv.2013.29.issue-1/anv-2013-0007/anv-2013-0007.pdf. Interview with Bishop Geoff Davies.

of sustainable development led to changes in activism: for example, more and more faith-based NGO managers are being trained in fundraising for the organisation's operations, and in the implementation of development projects in cooperation with public administration bodies and even with intergovernmental organisations. They also have to grasp the legal and technical character of international agreements such as the Kyoto Protocol and the Paris Agreement, for example. In the case of SAFCEI, it has designed a faith leader training programme (FLEAT), of which the main objective is to empower civil society through education and the advocacy of faith leaders in order to "be able to create a sustainable future, which prioritises affordable energy for all".[26]

The construction of a professional field of development implies that users as well as public authorities can draw on the expertise of faith-based NGOs. It is therefore necessary to know what their fields of expertise in climate action are. Is it, for example, expertise in getting populations to adapt to climate change? For SAFCEI and its FLEAT programme, the different actions put in place in different African countries such as training community members in organic farming in Zambia, running schools programme of talks on protecting the environment in Kenya, organising workshops for youth on climate change and poverty in Tanzania, are all rooted in the need for environmental education.

The advances of economic liberalism and democratisation along with the disengagement of the state offer new structures of opportunities to religious associations to engage with climate changes issues in the public interest and in line with the principles of participatory democracy. In order to benefit from these opportunities, the current public actions of faith-based actors presupposes that the state is engaging in open negotiations with multiple economic and social actors, as well as the decompartmentalisation of the public and private spheres, leading to public–private partnerships. Thus, instead of reflecting on new forms of polarisation between the state and the civil sector, should we not rather focus on the cooperation between the state and faith-based organisations? There are well-understood interests on both sides that need to be studied in order to comprehend both the "state relief" mechanisms as well as the growing cooperation between political institutions and faith-based NGOs.

---

[26] See more on FLEAT, https://safcei.org/project/fleat/.

This concrete relations-based political sociology thus serves the study of the model of citizenship perceived as the "structure of political opportunities", which is as much a political-institutional order as it is a cultural and discursive system.[27] In this respect, it is a matter of considering the national idea—which underlies the citizen identity disseminated jointly by citizens and religious leaders, the government elite, NGOs, trade unions—as the product of intense political work aimed at building or strengthening a unified collective identity. Faith-based NGOs, by engaging in environmental activities presented as a moral, religious and civic obligation, thereby contribute to the construction of a pluralist society and a religious citizenship that aims at creating universally adopted principles. This religious citizenship, which reveals religious practices and negotiations, and which has the capacity to generate meaning, refuses to cut itself off from its other various allegiances: national, local and community.

SAFCEI and the Concept of an Eco-Congregation

Mobilisation for the formation of an eco-congregation (mono- or multi-faith) is the result of the work of legitimisation, organisation and appropriation of material and human resources by actors who engage in collective actions.[28] This is why the means of communication and propagation are interesting to study. SAFCEI has been able to publicise its actions by having "recruited" persons from different faith organisations and church denominations in order to make itself known to the general public. The image they convey of themselves to society as a whole and the procedures they adopt for publicising environmental causes[29] contribute to the formation of an eco-congregation, new modes of political participation and pro-climate citizenship.

It is important to be aware of the evolution of social relations and the transformation of environmental actions in complex and dynamic socio-political configurations in a context of democratisation and religious

---

[27] M. Giugni, *Entre stratégie et opportunité: les mouvements sociaux en Suisse*, Zurich, Seismo, 1995.

[28] J.D. McCarthy & M.N. Zald, *Social Movements in an Organizational Society*, New Brunswick, Transaction Books, 1987.

[29] (McCarthy & Zald 1987).

pluralism such as in South Africa.[30] In other words, the analysis of social networks will shed light on the set of adjustments being constructed by SAFCEI in order to solve the concrete problems of its relations with its different partners within the government and with civil society. For example, on the level of interfaith dialogue, SAFCEI has supported a programme of social inclusiveness through the role of the Faith Leader Liaison for SAFCEI, who is also Chairperson of the Cape Town Interfaith Initiative and who graduated from One Spirit Interfaith Seminary in New York as an ordained Interfaith/Interspiritual Minister.[31]

Religious mobilisation for the environment and community development cannot develop without inter-religious and inter-community action. Both are very often embodied in ecumenical organisations already operating in the Christian field. The pro-environment community that is emerging in the quest for climate justice for the most vulnerable also tends to make denominations invisible. However, it is interesting to notice that Freire developed his interdisciplinary theory of education, engagement and development in an ecumenical organisation, the WCC in Geneva. It is worth remembering that the WCC played a significant role in the struggle against apartheid in South Africa by welcoming members and supporters of the ANC into its membership. Freire himself benefited from the solidarity of the WCC, which welcomed him as early as 1970 after he was forced to flee the dictatorial regime in Brazil. For ten years, he was the education advisor to this international ecumenical organisation.

---

[30] Important scientific literature is dedicated to religious pluralism and its legal treatment in South Africa: P. Fourie, "The SA Constitution and Religious Freedom: Perverter or Preserver of Religion's Contribution to the Public Debate on Morality?", *Scriptura*, 82 (1), 2003, pp. 94–107; G. Schyff, *The Limitation of the Rights to Freedom of Religion in South Africa*, Johannesburg, RAU, 2001; K. Henrad, "The Accommodation of Religious Diversity in South Africa Versus the Background of the Centrality of the Equality Principle in the New Constitutional Dispensation", *Journal of African Law*, 45 (1), 2001, pp. 51–72; N. Smith, "Freedom of Religion Under the Final Constitution", *South African Law Journal*, 1997; L. S. Underkuffer-Freund, "Religious Guarantees in a Pluralistic Society: Values, Problems and Limits", *South African Public Law*, 1997.

[31] Interview with Bishop Geoff Davies. The Faith Leader Liaison for SAFCEI is Rev Berry Behr. See about Rev Berry Behr, https://www.goldininstitute.org/our-team/63-2021-goldin-global-fellows/985-rev-berry-behr.

SAFCEI's Political Relations

Religious citizenship embodied in faith-based NGOs can also be at the service of a new stage of political liberalisation leading to the democratisation of public spaces and political institutions. Faith-based NGOs represent the new religious citizen movements in the public space of the new South Africa. But what about their action at the economic level? SAFCEI has been able to denounce the state's economic and industrial policies through legal challenges brought through cases related to the construction of nuclear power plants,[32] for example. In fact, a case brought jointly by SAFCEI and Earthlife Africa led to a court decision (Western Cape High Court) on 26 April 2017 rescinding the South African government's agreements with Russia, the United States and South Korea for the construction of eight nuclear power plants. This anti-nuclear campaign was also aimed at denouncing corruption in the country's energy sector during Jacob Zuma's presidency. This is but one example of the activities initiated by SAFCEI, whose political, social and economic pursuits are clearly recognised by the administrative authorities of the country.

With regard to political institutions and official religious organisations, we can ask whether NGOs such as SAFCEI are serving the climate cause from a state of dependency, or do they act as autonomous actors? The question is whether and to what extent the uses of religious citizenship reflect the autonomy of these civil society actors, considered as more than mere appendages of the public authorities. Moreover, do such NGOs represent a response to both national and international institutional stimuli? It is the process of politicisation that should be identified by insisting in particular on analysing the relations of negotiation, cooperation and even conflicts with the state. SAFCEI tends to make choices in order to satisfy expectations specific to a given context (cultural, political, socio-economic).[33] As a partner in top-down governance, religious actors who are members of SAFCEI are encouraged to use internal and external resources to create organisations and programmes to promote sustainable

---

[32] "South Africa's nuclear deals unlawful, court rules": https://www.bbc.com/news/world-africa-39717401, consulted on 16/12/2019. See also *SAFCEI* website: https://safcei.org/project/anti-nuclear-campaign/.

[33] J. March & J. Olsen, "The New Institutionalism: Organizational Factors in Political Life", *American Political Science Review*, 78, 1984, pp. 734–749.

development. However, such partnerships also evince tensions and even a willingness of faith-based NGOs such as SAFCEI to find a third way in the exercise of their political religiosity. They seek to work in sovereign independence without cutting themselves off from their close relations with the state and its representatives. In short, this process of gaining independence is action at a distance. In the case of SAFCEI, therefore, we are dealing with a critical public–private partnership without, of course, prejudging the risks of parastatal status that NGOs can face when they ultimately serve primarily the interests of states after having been created at the initiative of the state. Cooperative governance, multi-level governance, in the case of SAFCEI, is predominantly critical. Its links with international institutions (like IGOs such as UNDP, universities) but also with individuals such as Prof. Wangari Maathai, the Kenyan environmental activist and Nobel Peace Prize winner, and the strong social networks of religious organisations, represent strong capacities which enable SAFCEI to be an important stakeholder in the discussions with the state.

This religious citizenship embodied by SAFCEI in the field of environmental protection is expressed in a context of "deferred democracy"[34] that should be emphasised. Delayed democracy is a term used in both intellectual circles and by political opponents of the ANC to denounce the social injustices that continue to deepen social inequalities in the new South Africa.

In the broad and interwoven context of religious globalisation, political liberalisation and economic neoliberalism, SAFCEI as a multi-faith NGO is also affected, influenced by the challenges of the economic revolution that political opponents of the ANC and other civil society bodies are calling for. SAFCEI, because of its objective of addressing climate change, deals with the whole range of environmental problems and is also focused on the related issue of citizens' vulnerabilities.

Democracy and the Issue of Social Inequalities

It is common in South African intellectual circles to see the challenges of post-apartheid South Africa as related to the evolution of the ANC and its modes of governance; the ANC considers itself the oldest and

[34] (Gevisser 2007).

best known of the African liberation movements from which one of the world's leading figures, Nelson Mandela, emerged. Thus, a consensus emerges regarding the democratisation of the country linked to the ANC's evolution. The ANC played a major role in the successful transition from an apartheid regime to a democratic post-apartheid regime without unleashing major conflict. While led by the ANC, this post-apartheid political system nevertheless continues to legitimise the process of identifying South Africans along racial lines. For many, academics and political activists, what prevails beyond racial identification today is a continuity of a hard capitalism and a partial social transformation that has not only failed to reduce social inequalities but continues to reflect racial cleavages. In short, the ANC is often criticised for not having sufficiently protected the most vulnerable of the South African population in particular, but for sustaining a condition of deferred democracy.[35]

Booysen[36] sees the ANC as a hybrid "party-movement" that retains the capacity to connect with the people as a liberation movement,[37] as distinct from the conventional definition of a political party that nevertheless seeks through the rhetoric of its leaders to lead a "national democratic revolution", as the ANC puts it, and, according to Roger Southall, a quasi-theological one.[38] However, others[39] consider that political life within the ANC, plagued as it is by social class tensions and conflicts, is linked to the neoliberal economic context. Through this, thesis of the continuity of the domination of neoliberal principles in post-apartheid South Africa, what is at stake is the issue of the ANC being in power and its involvement in the "delayed or betrayed" revolution, but also of the possible advent of a social democracy.[40] The liberation of South Africa

---

[35] See Laurence Piper, "Crise, histoire et défi de la reinvention post-coloniale: l'African National Congress après l'apartheid", Politique africaine, n°134, June 2014, pp. 195–209.

[36] Susan Booysen, The African National Congress and... op. cit.

[37] Cited by Laurence Piper (Piper 2014: 205).

[38] R. Southall, "The ANC: Party Vanguard of the Black Middle Class?", in A. Lissoni et al. (A. Lissoni et al. 2012: 325).

[39] John Saul, "Globalisation, Recolonisation and the Paradox of Liberation in Southern Africa", in A. Lissoni et al. (eds), One Hundred Years of the ANC... (A. Lissoni et al. 2012: 347–366).

[40] See also Adam Habib, South Africa's Suspended Revolution. Hopes and Prospects, Johannesburg, Wits University Press, 2013.

was meant to lead not only to an end to the racially based political regime and systemic racism, but also bring to an end the neoliberal economic regime embodied in capitalist exploitation. It is widely acknowledged that the advent of democracy in 1994 did not bring about significant economic changes and many question the compromises made in the political negotiations to end apartheid, particularly those negotiated with former prisoner Mandela, which "delayed" or "betrayed" the liberation of the most vulnerable.[41] The thesis of a political-economic continuity is strongly supported by John Saul in opposition to the view that 1994 represented a new political point of departure. For Booysen, however, it is also important to stress the importance of the economic policies put in place by the ANC, which faced the challenge of having to resolve the country's difficult integration into the globalised economy while redressing the vast racial inequalities of the past through Black Economic Empowerment (BEE).[42]

All of these debates thus help to avoid understanding post-apartheid social changes only in political terms, even though they were clearly deeper than only economic changes.[43] Southall demonstrates that poverty was reduced for all but that, for example, during the early years of the ANC government, the black upper-middle class benefited more from the political and economic changes than the middle class did, and a new category of working poor developed by surviving in the informal employment sector. Thus political liberation did not lead to a radical democracy—which, in Habermas' view of radical democracy, is based on solidarity among members of society—as the ANC government saw growing inequality as a result of increased unemployment or precarious employment. The Black Economic Empowerment (BEE) policies, which sought to racially transform capital by letting black business people access the corporate sector, have been only moderately successful, since the lives of the majority of the population have not really changed. The political party has compensated for this by adopting a policy of social benefits for the poorest—who make up a large part of the ANC electorate—but without providing solutions for social transformation in the medium or

---

[41] (Piper 2014).

[42] (Southall 2012: 339). See also, G. Genre-Grandpierre, "Le Black Economic Empow-erment en Afrique du Sud: fondements, contraintes et risques", *Afrique contemporaine*, n°210, 2004/2, pp. 95–108.

[43] (Southall 2012: 325–346).

long term. This is therefore the second important point addressed in the literature on the state, democracy and the ANC in South Africa: economic change and its repercussions in terms of raised standards of living and income have essentially affected only that part of the population that has benefited from the BEE.

For Sampie Terreblanche,[44] the richest have continued to get richer and the poorest of the poor have continued to get poorer. Clearly, there is a context of asymmetrical transformation in South Africa. The political rupture characterised by the four-year transition from apartheid to the new South Africa, from Mandela's liberation in February 1990 to his democratic election as head of state in 1994, has not been followed by radical economic and social change. Thus, the economic liberation promised by the "democratic national revolution" in the era of neoliberal globalisation has not materialised. Should the emergence of a black upper-middle class be considered a radical social transformation? The poorest social strata, to which the refugees from the African continent belong, have not, according to Terreblanche's analysis, benefited from the ANC's economic policies.

This daunting economic and socio-political context makes it possible to understand in part the stakes involved in an eco-congregation, which is based on interfaith and intercultural dialogue and communicational action. The religious citizenship embodied by SAFCEI in the field of sustainable development and climate change becomes a new form of social and political affirmation of the actors of civil society in the context of a state marked by the condition of deferred democracy. It will therefore be interesting to question democracy and the way in which it influences the different forms of political construction of religious citizenship—in short, to investigate whether or not these models of associative engagement in the public space are new or not, and what their political and cultural consequences are compared to different forms of democratic regime. The fight against poverty has been globalised through the discourse of religious actors in their mobilisation for the climate in multilateral forums (see Chapter 4). However, it is at the local context such as new South Africa, one of the most unequal societies in the world, that we can observe the challenges of environmental activism: saving the planet

---

[44] Sampie Terreblanche, "La démocratie post-apartheid: un nouveau système élitiste ?", *Afrique contemporaine*, n°210, 2004, pp. 25–34. See also S. Terreblanche, *A History of Inequality in South Africa 1652–2002*, University of KwaZulu-Natal Press, 2002.

means primarily saving social cohesion and reimagining democracy.[45] Does the current international system marked by neoliberalism in the global economy enable this?

[45] Aysem Mert, "Challenges to Democracy in the Anthropocene", in D. Chandler et al. (eds.), *International Relations in the Anthropocene. New Agendas, New Agencies and New Approaches*, Palgrave Macmillan, 2021.

CHAPTER 6

Conclusion: Towards Convergence

Climate change, climate action and climate justice are related to various themes associated with environmental conservation, sustainable development, humanitarian aid, security and peace. The plea of religious actors for a sustainable world that takes into account climate justice (justice between people and different regions of the world, but also justice between generations), the value of biodiversity (justice towards non-human species through protection and conservation) and the role of scientific expertise in decision-making represents a cosmopolitan form of religious transnationalism. The discourse and actions of these religious actors serve to reinforce a transnational mobilisation for the global public good in cooperation with all the climate actors and represented by, for instance, interfaith action. They also give a sound basis to multi-level governance, which also influences debates on democracy and participatory democracy. Strengthening democratic practices and institutions within the state and implementation of rules such as the ones of the Paris Agreement are key challenges for any non-state actor. So non-state actors as well as states need to find a path for cooperation based on agreed norms. This path of cooperation seems to be embodied today in the UN's Sustainable Development Goals (SDG). The first sustainable development objectives were discussed internationally and adopted nearly half century ago with the first Earth Summit—the 1972 United Nations Conference on the

© The Author(s), under exclusive license to Springer Nature Switzerland AG 2022
S. Sadouni, *Religious Transnationalism and Climate Change,*
Human Rights Interventions,
https://doi.org/10.1007/978-3-031-10610-1_6

Human Environment—which recognised the need to protect the natural and cultural heritage. This led in the same year to the adoption of the World Heritage Convention by the UNESCO General Conference.

Within the international system, religious climate action is as a matter of fact linked to a liberal international order based on interdependence and inter-state cooperation, but also on cooperation between states and non-state actors. This last principle of international cooperation is clearly stipulated in the SDGs (Goal 17, "partnerships for the goals") and in the Paris Agreement, whose implementation was expected by 2020. The liberal values circulating in the context of the governance of climate change are related to respect for human rights, religious tolerance, solidarity, security and policies to fight poverty in accordance with the expertise of scientists, who point out that the risks of climate change are unevenly distributed across countries and that it is the poor, the most destitute, who will be the first victims in developing countries. These are also moral principles that religious actors wish to defend together. They wish to do so in a universal, rational discourse and within the framework of pragmatic action that nevertheless remains marked by the secularisation of international relations. The latter is the one likely to transcend social borders and to serve their action in favour of humanity and the protection of the planet.

Furthermore, this study of religious actors, as non-state actors, in the transnational field of climate action illustrates how the circulation of their beliefs and moral value can contribute to a "moral order". In order to achieve sustainable development—meaning a global economy that is prosperous, socially inclusive and environmentally sustainable—an implementation of treaties framed for the common good is needed: good governance of global public goods implemented locally and internationally at the same time. The Glasgow Climate Pact from the recent COP 26 mentions the following principle: "multilevel and cooperative action", but without any mention of the "governance":

> Recognizing the important role of indigenous peoples, local communities and civil
> society, including youth and children, in addressing and responding to climate change, and highlighting the urgent need for multilevel and cooperative action.

Even though religious actors do not explicitly mention world citizenship, an allegiance to the planet is somehow implicit in their discourse in the sense and form of "*Kosmu polites*".[1] However, this study has shown that the highest priority they express is towards fellow human beings, especially for those in a vulnerable situation, the poor. These non-state actors do not ask for a new form of (political) loyalty, but what transpires instead in their discourse and statements before the COPs, and in support of human rights, is a strict allegiance to humanity based on religious beliefs and moral values. The issue of non-human species, which was briefly mentioned here, is still a field of research to be explored in order to understand and analyse the stance of religious actors and interfaith actions on the approach to protect biodiversity and all life on the planet. This development that can be expected in the future as national and international policies targeting the mitigation of global warming are at the heart of a universal discourse on the environment and climate change that dates back to the 1970s—the need to save the planet, including the beings who reside on it.

The perspective of international political sociology adopted here sought also to analyse the practices and interactions of actors in international relations (state and non-state) within multilateral frameworks. UN international conferences are the place where these interactions can describe force and power relationships. However, these power relationships are also dependent on state capacity to adopt pro-environmental legislation within a system of cooperative governance. The nature of strength or weakness in state capacity needs to be analysed in the local context. These complex internal and external contexts need to be addressed simultaneously with regard to legislation and institutional solutions for climate adaptation and mitigation. Climate policies, like any other policies, need targets and objectives but their implementation also requires social activism. One wonders if religious and church leaders do not have a higher capacity to undertake climate action and advocacy because of the nature of their institutions, compared to secular activists who after launching environmental initiatives move into government and consultancies. The lack of autonomy and economic independence of environmental activists can indeed weaken civic structures and contribute to

---

[1] M. Ayaz Naseem & Emery J. Hyslop-Margison, "Nussbaum's Concept of Cosmopolitanism: Practical Possibility or Academic Delusion?", *Paideusis*, 15 (2), 2006, pp. 51–60.

their social and political marginalisation.[2] The Roman Catholic Church and especially the Vatican has a sovereign juridical entity under international law: the Holy See. It is the government and the diplomatic representative of the Roman Catholic Church and operates from the Vatican City State, a sovereign territory. This diplomatic institutional dimension can give permanence to the capacity of the Catholic Church to influence transnational and international mobilisation for climate action.

Religious actors are well placed to arrange a convergence of beliefs, a sense of community belonging and environmentally oriented practice in the process of transnational climate action based on their moral authority and legitimacy. Action to promote democracy, human rights and the protection of the planet is growing in all the sectors of civil society, nationally and internationally. However, the religious actors who focus simultaneously on repentance[3]—change of mind—have adopted a critical stance towards a neoliberal globalisation considered as a channel that can lead to the degradation of the environment through global warming and to increasing individualism with materialist concerns. Moral economy through moral action can encompass this dialectical dimension of religious transnationalism in the field of climate action: promoting a cosmopolitan view of the world through the protection of human rights and the planet but at the same time advocating for a transformation based on repentance.

Assessing religious climate action in participative or exclusionary policy targeting climate mitigation and sustainable development depends more on the analysis of the local, national context. This will help to answer the question about the kind of power religious actors have to exert an influence on the local and on their congregation. However, on the international scene, and in the transnational field of climate action studied here, international norms of cooperation with religious actors and faith-based organisations are central in the circulation of their discourse and actions. And this remains a social fact that political sociology cannot deny even in international relations.

---

[2] J. Cock & D. Fig, "The Impact of Globalization on Environmental Politics in South Africa, 1990–2002", *African Sociological Review*, 5 (2), 2001, pp. 15–35.

[3] *Metanoia* in terms of repentance and change is the term used in Christian and the WCC circles for change. See G. Kerber, "International advocacy for climate justice", in R. Globus Veldman, A. Szasz & R. Haluza-DeLay, *How the World's Religions are Responding to Climate Change: Social Scientific Investigations*, London, Routledge, 2016, p. 292.

INDEX

A

Adaptation, 7, 16, 33, 35, 46, 48, 49, 55, 56, 62, 69, 70, 72, 93
Africa, 12, 13, 32, 33, 37, 44, 55, 64, 76, 80, 85
African National Congress (ANC), 71, 73–79, 84, 86–89
All Africa Conference of Churches (AACC), 33, 44
Alliance of Religions and Conservation (ARC), 29, 55, 63, 64
Annan, Kofi, 61
Anthropocene, 3, 4, 49, 57
Anthropogenic, 1, 9, 36, 53
Assisi, 55

B

Beck, Ulrich, 4, 9, 11, 16, 17, 19, 21
Biodiversity, 25, 32, 34, 35, 61, 91, 93

C

Carbon market, 45, 46, 49
China, 12, 35, 43, 44, 46, 48, 64, 66
Climate change, 1–4, 6–10, 12, 15–18, 20–24, 32–35, 38–40, 42–44, 46, 48, 52–54, 56–63, 65, 67, 68, 72, 80–82, 86, 89, 91–93
Common goods, 8, 35, 68, 80, 81, 92
Conference of the Parties (COP), 6, 7, 17, 35–39, 41–43, 46–49, 53, 55–59, 92, 93
Convergence, 94
Cosmopolitan, 4, 8, 11, 15, 16, 19–24, 51, 57, 91, 94

D

Dalai Lama, 62, 68, 69
Democracy, 17, 72, 73, 82, 86–91, 94
Divestment, 39

Durkheim, 16, 72

E

Eco-congregation, 72, 73, 79–81, 83, 89
Ecumenical Patriarch, Patriarch Bartholomew I of Constantinople, 46, 53
Ethical, 3, 7, 8, 12, 19, 21, 30, 51, 52, 58, 60, 62, 63, 67
  ethic, 13, 27, 51, 65, 67, 69, 70, 81

F

Faith for Earth, 17, 23, 59, 67
Figueres, Christiana, 61
Fossil fuels, 33, 38, 39, 56, 58, 63–66
Freire, Paulo, 72, 80, 84

G

Giddens, Anthony, 36, 46, 64, 67
Glasgow Climate Pact, 35, 92
Globalisation, 2, 11, 13, 20, 36, 37, 86, 89, 94
Global public good, 37, 39, 91, 92
Governance, 2, 3, 9, 16, 23, 25, 33, 34, 70, 78, 85, 86, 92, 93
  multi-level governance, 7, 23, 52, 63, 67, 86, 91
Green Fund, 49, 69, 70
Guterres, Antonio, 61

H

Habermas, J., 72, 88
Hessel, Stéphane, 68, 69
Human rights, 4, 29, 59, 60, 69, 78, 92–94
Huntington, Samuel P., 14, 30

I

Indigenous populations, 36
Inequality, 7, 12, 16, 29, 54, 86–88
Interfaith liaison committee (ILC), 53, 56, 57
Intergovernmental, 2, 3
  intergovernmental organisations (IGO), 5, 61, 73
Intergovernmental Panel on Climate Change (IPCC), 1, 8, 9, 36, 40, 42, 48
International Union for Conservation of Nature (IUCN), 35
Inter-religious dialogue, 22
Islamic declaration on climate change, 58, 64
Islamic Foundation for Ecology and Environmental Sciences (IFEES), 17, 40

J

Justice, 8, 57, 78, 79, 91
  climate justice, 7, 12, 29, 37, 49, 50, 53, 57, 59, 63, 66, 70, 72, 84, 91
  social justice, 4, 13, 16, 80

K

Ki Moon, Ban, 59, 60, 68
Kyoto Protocol, 8, 23, 33, 38, 40, 42–49, 82

L

Legislation, 6, 93

M

Mandela, Nelson, 74, 75, 77–79, 87–89
Migrant refugees, 34

Mitigation, 3, 6, 7, 16, 19, 23, 35, 38, 43, 46, 48, 49, 62, 66, 67, 69, 70, 72, 93, 94
Mizan, Al-Mizan A Covenant for the Earth, 17, 47
Moral, 2–5, 8, 9, 29, 38, 51–53, 55, 57, 59, 61, 62, 65, 67, 80, 83, 92–94
Moral economy, 72, 80, 94
Multilateralism, 2, 11, 41
multilateral, 2, 3, 7–10, 13, 15, 18, 24, 36, 40, 41, 43, 44, 48, 51, 53, 55, 57, 58, 68, 89, 93
Muslim Judicial Council (MJC), 34, 35

N
Nationally Determined Commitments, 66
Non-governmental organisation (NGO), 8, 14, 17–19, 24, 26, 27, 31, 32, 37, 42, 47, 52, 56, 63, 67, 71–73, 79, 81–83, 85, 86

O
Organisation of Islamic Cooperation, 47

P
Paris Agreement, 1, 3–5, 12, 35, 37, 41–43, 46, 47, 49, 56, 60–62, 66, 69, 82, 91, 92
Peace, 8, 13, 14, 21, 22, 33, 55, 57, 69, 76, 80, 86, 91
Pope Francis, 25, 54, 57, 63, 68
Pope John Paul II, 55
Poverty, 7, 8, 11–13, 16, 27, 29, 33, 47, 51, 57, 59, 60, 80, 82, 88, 89, 92
poor, 12, 57

Prevention, 62, 79
Prince Philip, 55

R
Religions for Peace, 56, 62, 67
Repentance, 47, 94

S
Sachs, Jeffrey D., 25, 51, 59, 61, 62, 70
Secularisation, 2, 14, 62
Security, 5, 8, 13, 33, 37, 54, 80, 91, 92
Social action, 52
Solidarity, 13, 16, 37, 55, 62, 67, 72, 78, 84, 88, 92
South Africa, 3, 6, 17, 28, 34, 39, 44, 45, 56, 70–81, 84–87, 89
Southern African Faith Communities' Environment (SAFCEI), 17, 19, 71–73, 79–86, 89
Stern, Nicholas, 38, 61
Sustainable development, 1, 3–5, 7, 12, 22, 23, 25, 26, 32–34, 40, 41, 49, 51, 52, 57, 62, 63, 67, 68, 70, 72, 80, 81, 86, 89, 91, 92, 94

T
Tolerance, 21, 29, 67, 80, 92
Transnational climate field/transnational field of climate change, 5, 7, 19, 20, 22, 50, 70, 72
Tubiana, Laurence, 35

U
United Nations Conference on the Human Environment, 41, 92

United Nations Development
    Programme (UNDP), 60, 63, 71,
    79, 80, 86

United Nations Environment
    Programme (UNEP), 8, 17, 23,
    41, 42, 59, 67

United Nations Framework
    Convention on Climate Change
    (UNFCCC), 2, 3, 6, 7, 15, 17,
    33, 37, 38, 40–42, 44, 46, 48,
    49, 53, 55, 56, 58, 59, 61, 66

United Nations Sustainable
    Development Goals (SDG), 5,
    34, 91

W
World Bank, 12, 27–30, 32, 38, 61
World Council of Churches (WCC),
    39, 40, 47, 53–56, 59, 60, 66,
    84, 94
World Faith Development Dialogue
    (WFDD), 27
World Wildlife Fund (WWF), 54, 55,
    63

The manufacturer's authorised representative in the EU is Springer Nature Customer Service Centre GmbH, Europaplatz 3, 69115 Heidelberg, Germany. If you have any concerns regarding our products, please contact ProductSafety@springernature.com

Printed and bound by CPI Group (UK) Ltd, Croydon, CR0 4YY
24/04/2026
02096315-0007